LIVING WITH BUGS

Living with Bugs

Least-Toxic Solutions to Everyday Bug Problems

Jack DeAngelis

with drawings by Elizabeth A. DeAngelis

Oregon State University Press Corvallis

The paper in this book meets the guidelines for permanence and durability of the Committee on Production Guidelines for Book Longevity of the Council on Library Resources and the minimum requirements of the American National Standard for Permanence of Paper for Printed Library Materials Z39.48-1984.

Library of Congress Cataloging-in-Publication Data

DeAngelis, Jack D.
  Living with bugs : least-toxic solutions to everyday bug problems / Jack D. DeAngelis ; with drawings by Elizabeth A. DeAngelis.
     p. cm.
  Includes index.
  ISBN 978-0-87071-421-4 (alk. paper)
  1. Urban entomology. I. Title.
  QL472.7.D43 2009
  648'.7--dc22

                                                        2009003687

Text design: Steve Connell

First published in 2009 by Oregon State University Press
Printed in the United States of America

Oregon State University Press
121 The Valley Library
Corvallis OR 97331-4501
541-737-3166 • fax 541-737-3170
http://oregonstate.edu/dept/press

Table of Contents

Introduction

I have been studying insects, mites, and similar critters for thirty years and find them endlessly fascinating. I write about them on my website and blog, and I photograph them whenever I remember to bring a camera along on an outing. I realize, however, that not everyone shares this fascination. In fact, most people are at least somewhat—and sometimes very—fearful of anything creepy-crawly. This book will be a success if I convince you, gentle reader, that nearly all insects, spiders, mites, and their allies are harmless and even beneficial—they all play critical roles in the Earth's biological systems. A very small number are potentially harmful, but even these can be managed in safe and responsible ways that minimize their damage potential while not hurting anything else, including yourself. A few, of course, are *truly annoying!* That's what this book is for—to sort the good critters from the bad and the truly annoying ones.

I began my studies of entomology working on spider mites at New Mexico State University in the mid-1970s. That interest lead me to Oregon State University, where I continued working on spider mites and the damage they do to crop plants, the subject of my doctoral thesis. I left OSU for a time to work with a forest entomologist at Mississippi State University, then did a stint at North Carolina State University working on the state's insect survey program from 1985 to 1988. I finally returned to OSU in the late 1980s and remained there as an extension urban entomologist until my retirement in 2004.

About the book

This book is about the insects, and similar critters, that people love to hate. There are many millions of different insect species in the world, plus an equally large number of organisms that are related to insects. Of all these varied forms and life histories, only a small number are noticed by the average person. Those species that get noticed by non-scientists are generally large, colorful, noisy, annoying, destructive, or dangerous; *ninety-nine percent of all insects are none of these things.*

Almost twenty years of answering questions from the public has taught me that a few insects, mites, and other topics are universally important to homeowners. These are the subjects of this book. Some of the topics covered may not pertain to where you live. For example, unless you live in the southern US you probably have never encountered a fire ant. You are allowed, if you wish, to skip these parts and save them for future reference—say, when you get transferred to Mississippi.

We'll cover critters that bite; some that damage buildings; some that are aggressive; some that try to share our food or clothing; a couple that get under our skin; and some imaginary types, too; big biting flies; "nuisance" house guests; some venomous spiders; and various related subjects. With a few exceptions, I have intentionally not mentioned particular trade names of pest-control products; these names change so often that to do so would quickly render the book outdated. Fortunately the Internet provides a way to update this kind of information in a quick and timely way. For specific pest-control information, go to the relevant pages at **LivingWithBugs.com**, this book's companion website.

Some people have told me they like the title of our website and this book, *Living with Bugs*, but others have said they don't. Some have told me they don't like the idea of living with bugs in any shape or form! Others tell me they like the title, because it says to them that we can learn to coexist with "bugs" and not always have to think about simply exterminating them. I like this second interpretation. In fact, we are *not* in direct competition with most insects for either space or resources. A few eat our crops or otherwise damage our food or possessions, a few infect us with diseases, sometimes deadly diseases, but for the most part insects don't negatively impact people to any great extent in modern society. With a little effort we can learn to appreciate insects—or at least just to ignore them, since most of the time they won't bother us if we don't bother them.

Why do bugs exist?

After carefully explaining the life history of some insect, I'm sometimes asked: "*So what's it good for?*" This question always strikes me as odd, and I have difficulty answering it. I assume that the questioner is asking something like: "*So how does this insect make* my *life better*"? Without starting a long philosophical debate, let me just say that I believe that insects—and all living organisms on planet Earth—are here because they fill an ecological niche, not to serve mankind in some way. Organisms exist because there's space for them in the fabric of life. If, for example, the lowly bed bug does not seem to be doing *us* any good, it is only because it is not. In fact, *we serve its purposes far more than it serves ours*!

Who is this book written for?

The book is written mainly for homeowners and renters, and those who support them, such as Master Gardeners and other Cooperative Extension folks. I worked for Cooperative Extension as an Extension Entomology Specialist for sixteen years and taught classes for Master Gardeners from many counties throughout Oregon. I can attest to the value Master Gardener volunteers add to Extension's mission. I've included information in the Appendix about how to contact your local county Extension office.

Even though I've written this book for non-entomologists, I have not avoided difficult terms and concepts like insect taxonomy, pesticide resistance, parasites, and so on. Wherever possible

Google as a verb

Most of you probably know that **Google** is an Internet site and company that specializes in indexing the World Wide Web. If you navigate to the Google site (www.google.com), you can enter a **search term** or question and Google will search its index database and give you a list of sites that are relevant to your search. While there are many other search engines (sites that specialize in indexing the Internet), the act of searching at google.com is so universal these days that it has become a recognized verb: to google. Suggestions to "google" this or that to find further information can be found throughout the book. You are, of course, welcome to use your own favorite search engine site to explore these topics.

I've tried to cover these side issues in some detail. I urge you to google any terms you don't understand and also to take a look at the Internet references listed at the end of each section.

The measure of a bug—converting millimeters to inches

Descriptions of bugs often use the metric scale for measurements. The standard unit of the metric scale is the millimeter. The bug world is generally defined by the range of about 50 mm (2") down to about 1 mm ($\frac{1}{32}$"). Not too many insects or mites fall outside this range. An easy way to roughly convert millimeters to inches is to remember that **25 mm equals about 1 inch**. If, for example, the description says 2.5 mm, which is $\frac{1}{10}$ of 25, the equivalent measurement in inches is $\frac{1}{10}$". Here are some other equivalent measures:

1"	= 25.4 mm	~ diameter of a US quarter
¾"	~ 19.0 mm	~ diameter of a US penny
½"	~ 12.7 mm	~ diameter of the little finger of an average-size person
¼"	~ 6.4 mm	~ diameter of a standard #2 wood pencil
⅛"	~ 3.2 mm	~ height of the printed letters on this page
1⁄16"	~ 1.6 mm	~ diameter of a #2 pencil lead or thickness of a US penny
1⁄32"	~ 0.8 mm	~ size of a single grain of table salt

All insects are Arthropods but not all Arthropods are insects

The term Arthropod means "jointed-foot"; it includes all the animals that have an **exoskeleton,** or hard outer shell-like skeleton, and thus need to have a flexible joint between their body and leg segments in order to be able to move and bend. Without these joints, insects and their relatives would be awfully stiff-legged. Familiar examples of arthropods are insects, spiders, scorpions, crabs, lobsters, and all mites, including ticks. Because insects are the dominant group within the arthropods, scientists often use the terms **insects and related arthropods** or insects and their close relatives to refer to these groups.

Insect orders

Scientists group insects and other organisms by common external features. For example, if you put an ant next to a wasp next to a bee (see illustrations above), you'll notice some similarities that distinguish this group (called Hymenoptera)—such as 2 pairs of membranous wings (only the reproductive stages of ants have wings; see page 47), an abdomen constricted at base to form a sort of "waist," similar antennae, etc.—from other insects like beetles or flies.

All insects are grouped into one of approximately 30 different Orders. Many insect orders contain groups that are unfamiliar to non-entomologists. Only the orders most commonly encountered by homeowners are included in the following list:

Orthoptera—grasshoppers and crickets; nymphs are similar to adults but smaller and wingless

Dictyoptera—cockroaches; nymphs are similar to adults but smaller and wingless

Isoptera—termites; nymphs are similar to adults but smaller and wingless

Mallophaga—lice; nymphs are similar to adults and, like adults, feed on blood

Hemiptera—true bugs like bed bugs, boxelder bugs, stink bugs; nymphs are similar to adults but smaller and wingless

Homoptera—aphids and scale insects; nymphs are similar to adults but smaller and wingless

Coleoptera—beetles; larvae are called **grubs** and are worm-like, with or without legs

Hymenoptera—ants, wasps, bees; larvae are legless and worm-like

Lepidoptera—butterflies and moths; larvae, or **caterpillars**, are worm-like

Diptera—flies and mosquitoes; larvae of "higher" flies (house flies, cluster flies, etc.) are called **maggots**; the larvae of "primitive" flies (mosquito, midges, etc.) are usually aquatic or semi-aquatic

Siphonaptera—fleas; larvae are worm-like and do not bite

Is it a *larva* (plural = larvae) or a *nymph*?

There are many different names for immature insects. Depending on the group to which they belong, immature insects can be called maggots, grubs, caterpillars, larvae, nymphs, or naiads. **Larva** is a general term for an immature insect that *does not resemble the adult insect,* such as an immature beetle larva or **grub**. The term can also be used, however, to refer to any immature animal (a larval crab, for example). The term **nymph** is used to denote those groups of immature insects *whose immature stages closely resemble the adult stage,* such as grasshoppers.

Illustrations

A book like this one is often judged by the selection and quality of the illustrations. After all, you probably bought this book, at least in part, to be able **to identify what's bugging you**. You will find black and white photographs of the bugs with their descriptions and, where noted, also a color plate.

In the interests of space, and, of course, cost, I've only selected illustrations that show those life stages and species that are possibly less familiar; I've omitted those I felt were more commonly known. I have also omitted highly magnified images, because the average homeowner will never see this view. For example, I could have included an electron micrograph of the jaws, or *chelicerae*, of a spider. It is a beautiful image, but it is not much use to someone whose main interest is knowing whether or not that hairy spider in the corner is venomous. There are excellent picture books offering a magnified view of the insect world, if that is what you desire. One such book is *Amazing Insects: Images of Fascinating Creatures* by Michael Chinery (Firefly Books, 2008).

Pesticides

Pesticides are chemicals that kill or disrupt the activity of a pest. A pest is any living animal, plant, or microbe that we decide **causes a loss to something we value**, such as health or property (pretty self-righteous, huh?). By definition, then, pesticides are poisons, at least to some pest. More often, pesticides are **generally poisonous** to a wide range of organisms, and therefore **great care** should be taken in their use. Even products purchased at your local home and garden store must be handled carefully to avoid damage to you or your property. Always, *always* read the product label and always apply the **least amount** of the product that is effective. The old adage "*if a little is good, a lot must be better*" is definitely not applicable when it comes to pesticides.

The biggest mistake I see people make when using pesticides is what is called *misapplication*. A misapplication is either using the wrong chemical—for example, a weed killer intended for grasses may be *misapplied* to control a broadleaf weed—or using the correct chemical at the wrong time of year. You can avoid many misapplications by, again, carefully reading the label instructions for application timing and target pests.

Keep in touch

I can be easily reached through my website at LivingWithBugs.com. If my e-mail address changes, I'll always post the current address on the About Us page. I'm happy to answer e-mailed bug questions (though there's a small fee if you need something identified or diagnosed), and I'll gladly take comments about the book. I've also posted a page, www.livingwithbugs.com/bug_book.html, where you can find updates, corrections, and additional images.

Acknowledgments

Ken Gray (1905–1981) took many of the original images used throughout this book. Ken was an entomologist at Oregon State University and later worked for Pacific Supply Cooperative in Portland, Oregon. Between April 1964 and October 1976, while working for Pacific Supply, Ken produced a large collection of photographs of insects and related arthropods. His images can often be identified by the neutral gray background on which he placed his subjects. Sets of his images, as duplicate color slides, were distributed to universities and other governmental agencies in the late 1970s under an Environmental Protection Agency grant. I am grateful to his long dedication to the art of insect photography. The Ken Gray Image Collection can be searched online at www.ipmnet.org/kgphoto/.

An author needs anonymous reviewers to point out where and how a manuscript can be improved and I've been lucky to have had good ones. These reviews helped me in many ways, especially with suggestions about how to express this or that point in a better, clearer way. Reviewers, and you know who you are—I am grateful for your help. Surviving errors of omission or commission are of course mine, and mine alone.

The editors at OSU Press, and especially Mary Braun, have been wonderful to work with over the course of the planning and execution of this book. No author can do the enormous amount of detailed planning and scheduling work that the editors do, and do so well. Thank you.

Finally, my wife Elizabeth contributed her artistic talent in the drawings of various critters. She also added a great deal of information and drawings to the sections on identifying bugs and bug damage (pages 154-170). Furthermore, she edited early drafts of the manuscript and made important suggestions about content and layout. Thanks, Sweets!

Chapter 1
Critters that bite and leave a red, itchy bump

This chapter is about the insects (and a close relative of theirs) that get the most attention from homeowners—because *they bite.* Some insects bite, or sting, in their own defense, but the critters in this group bite in order to **feed on blood.** The bites often contain compounds that cause a red, itchy skin lesion around the bite mark. Sometimes these blood-feeders even inject microorganisms that **cause disease.** The critters in this group include **bed bugs, black flies, fleas, human lice, biting midges, mosquitoes,** and **ticks**.

In the US, mosquitoes and ticks are by far the most important members of this group in terms of the diseases they carry. Worldwide, mosquitoes are the most important disease carriers and are responsible for epidemics of **malaria, yellow fever, dengue fever**, and **West Nile fever,** to name just a few. Ticks have gained a lot of attention in the US over the last few years because certain ticks carry microorganisms that cause **Lyme disease** as well as a variety of other blood-borne diseases. In terms of human history, **fleas** have had a profound effect as well. Certain fleas carry microbes which can cause a pandemic disease called the **plague** or **black death.** Not to be outdone, **black flies** can infect their hosts with some pretty nasty diseases, too. A bite from a black fly in some tropical parts of the world can leave you with **onchocerciasis,** also known as "river blindness."

Deadly diseases are one thing, but let's face it—what most people hate are the **itchy bites** that critters in this group cause.

Itchy, swollen bites are caused by our bodies' reaction to chemicals left behind in the bites. People react differently to individual bites, and you may react differently to the same type of bite at different times. People also differ in how "attractive" they are to different pests. You probably know—and possibly even despise—someone who never seems to get a mosquito bite, while the little suckers attack *you* without mercy.

Bed bugs *(Cimex lectularius)*

The role of bed bugs in natural ecosystems: All bed bugs are ectoparasites of warm-blooded animals like birds, bats, and humans.

When our ancient, nomadic ancestors first moved into caves looking for shelter from the elements, they may have encountered small, blood-feeding insects. Before the arrival of these ancient peoples, such insects would have fed on the blood of cave-nesting bats and birds. Like any good "vampire," these insects fed at night while their hosts slept. The insects caused no real harm aside from some skin irritation and would have been hardly noticed by our rugged forebears.

Below: **bed bug** feeding (3.5x). Adult bugs are about ¼" long. Reproduced in color on Plate 1. Modified from Ken Gray Collection. Courtesy of Oregon State University (#392-6). Right: Hiding places, droppings and typical bites of bed bugs.

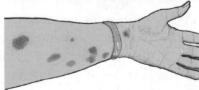

The insects our ancestors likely encountered were members of a group called Cimicidae, or the bed bugs. Bed bugs feed on the blood of birds and mammals. In humans their bites result in what appears to be a **severe mosquito-like bite**. Unlike mosquito bites, however, bed-bug bites do not generally cause disease. Bed bugs are small (⅕"–¼"), oval, wingless, reddish-brown colored insects. Immature, or larval, bed bugs are very similar in appearance to adults except for body size, but they are lighter in color.

Bed bugs belong to the insect genus *Cimex*, and there are a number of different species. One species has so closely adapted to feeding on modern humans that it has literally moved into our homes, motel rooms, and other shelters, and is found almost nowhere else; this species is *Cimex lectularius*. Bed bugs feed at night on a sleeping host and hide during the day in bedding and bedside furniture. Bed-bug bites are initially painless but later develop into localized swelling, redness, and an itchy lesion.

In the latter half of the 20th century, bed-bug infestations became relatively rare in most places. Why did this happen? The most direct cause was probably the frequent use indoors of **organophosphate** and **organochlorine** insecticides. These new classes of insecticide were developed during World War II to combat wartime epidemics and were considered a miracle cure for many pest insects and the diseases they carried. Such residual insecticides were very effective at suppressing and eliminating bed-bug infestations. In

Insecticide classes

Synthetic (manufactured) insecticides belong to various groups based on their chemical structure. These groups are called classes. Until fairly recently there were just four classes of synthetic insecticides: **organophosphates**, **organochlorines**, **carbamates**, and **pyrethroids**. This classification system is useful for predicting the characteristics of an insecticide, such as its toxicity and how persistent it might be in the environment. In recent years many new insecticide classes have sprung up.

fact, they were so effective that, in industrialized countries, most people born after 1945 have never encountered these critters. In the 1960s, however, spurred by the publication of Rachel Carson's landmark book, *Silent Spring,* scientists began to learn that these insecticides had a downside. Synthetic insecticides were found to cause damage to the environment; they also posed a significant danger to human health if not used properly.

Fast-forward to the 1980s: organochlorine and organophosphate insecticides began to be banned in the US for all indoor uses because of health concerns about residues from these compounds. As the insecticide residues disappeared from our living spaces, our old sleeping companion, the bed bug, staged a comeback. Bed-bug infestations first show up in high-traffic motels. Bed bugs move from place to place on the belongings of their hosts, so they may be transported in luggage and brought home. The second most frequent means of bed-bug travel is on discarded and reused furniture.

Since bed bugs are not important sources of human disease, our main concern is with their irritating bite, along with their potential to stigmatize commercial properties (motels, inns, and such). Because bed-bug infestations are still relatively rare, an outbreak is also cause for much negative media attention.

Bed-bug infestations can be safely managed by attention to cleaning and the use of low-toxicity, residual insecticides. Bedding should be laundered at least once a week. It is important to clean all mattress surfaces and seams, because these offer another place where bed bugs can hide. Clean bedside furniture and the bed frame, too, because this is often where bed bugs hide during the day. Finally, if an active infestation is found, treat mattress seams, and any cracks or crevices around the bed, with a low-toxicity insecticidal silica dust.

Treat bed-bug bites with over-the-counter antibiotic and anti-itch medications. Scratching a bed-bug bite can lead to a secondary skin infection which can end up being more serious than the original bite.

Checking a motel room for bed bugs

Motel rooms can be easily checked for bed bugs before you move in for the night. Lift up the corners of the bed sheets and look for **dark spots or stains** (bed-bug droppings) along the mattress seams. Next, run your fingers or a clean cloth along the underside edges of bedside tables and along the back edge of the headboard (if it is not attached to the wall). Look for bed-bug droppings or the bugs themselves in these places, too. Another indication of the presence of bed bugs is a **distinctive odor** produced by the bugs themselves. The odor is sometimes described as "sickly sweet," or even compared to the smell of fresh raspberries. The odor will only be detectable in a heavily infested room.

By the way, the spelling "bedbug," without a space between bed and bug, is incorrect; bed bug is the correct spelling. Since bed bugs are true bugs, belonging to the insect order Hemiptera, the "bed" part modifies the "bug" part. However, the "bedbug" spelling is widely used, even by some entomologists who should know better.

Internet resources:

www.livingwithbugs.com/bed_bug.html
www.hsph.harvard.edu/bedbugs/
www.ohioline.osu.edu/hyg-fact/2000/2105.html

Black flies (Simuliidae)

The role of black flies in natural ecosystems: Adult black flies are ectoparasites of warm-blooded animals, while black fly larvae live in freshwater streams as predators and scavengers.

Black flies are very small ($\frac{1}{16}$"–$\frac{1}{8}$"), usually dark-colored flies that may be common around flowing streams and rivers, where black fly larvae develop. Black flies can be fierce *daytime* biting

Black fly. Notice the "humpback" profile. These flies are sometimes called humpback flies or buffalo gnats. Drawing modified from Baker, Apperson, Arends 1986. AG-369

flies (in contrast to mosquitoes which usually bite in the morning or evening) and often occur in swarms. Bites can be quite painful and may bleed because of a strong anticoagulant injected at the bite site. Bites result in swelling and an intense itch. Black fly larvae are very sensitive to water pollution and can be used as indicators of water purity. Larvae attach themselves to submerged objects, such as rocks or vegetation, and feed by filtering small aquatic organisms, such as bacteria and algae, from the passing water. Black flies can be very significant livestock pests as well,

River blindness (onchocerciasis)

River blindness is caused by a parasitic worm, or nematode, that can live in the human body for many years. When certain black fly species bite, their saliva may contain larvae of these worms. Developing larvae can cause damage to the skin, but the real danger is when larvae migrate to the eyes and cause blindness (river blindness). Currently, river blindness and the skin aliments of onchocerciasis can be largely prevented with a drug called ivermectin. Merck & Co. Inc. manufactures the drug and has donated it for elimination of river blindness in poor and developing counties around the world. There are, however, already some reports of drug resistance to ivermectin. See www.en.wikipedia.org/wiki/River_blindness for more information.

sometimes resulting in fatalities if animals are not able to escape swarming flies. In addition, black fly swarms frequently disrupt recreational activities.

Black flies are typically more abundant in spring and early summer. Eggs are laid in water and hatched larvae attach themselves to underwater objects. Larvae develop through several stages, pupate under water, and emerge as adults, floating to the surface in a bubble of air. There may be multiple generations each year, especially in warm climates.

Black flies do not transmit disease in North America. In the tropics of South America and Africa a very serious disease called onchocerciasis, or "river blindness," is carried by certain black flies. Onchocerciasis is a leading infectious cause of blindness worldwide.

There's not much that homeowners can do to limit black fly numbers on their own. Some municipal entities have established control programs (for example www.depweb.state.pa.us/blackfly/

Insect repellents are really a kind of "cloaking device"

Star Trek fans will recall a Romulan device that made objects, even starships, invisible to their enemies. The devices were called "cloaking devices," and every respectable galactic warship had one. This is how insect repellents work, too. Repellents don't actually repel insects; instead they make you literally **invisible** to them. Certain insects—such as mosquitoes, black flies and biting midges—use odors our bodies produce to locate us. They home in on these odors, and if they are masked by repellents the insects can't find us. It's even better than this, in fact—if we don't smell right, they won't bite even if they accidentally bump into us.

Since the 1950s most insect repellents have been made from the chemical **DEET** (N,N'-diethyl-3-methylbenzamide). Maximum-strength repellents contain 100% DEET but some repellents use concentrations as low as 5%. DEET is an oily liquid that can be applied to skin or clothing (although it dissolves certain plastics ➤

➤ and synthetic fabrics). *Do not apply DEET directly to tent fabrics.* DEET is an effective "cloaking device" against ticks, mosquitoes, black flies, and biting midges. The concentration of DEET in a particular product largely determines how long the repellent effect will last. Concentrations of around 30% may provide as much as 8 hours of protection while lower concentrations provide progressively shorter protection times. The length of effectiveness does not seem to increase significantly with concentrations above 30%.

There are some reported health risks associated with heavy DEET use. Scientific studies have found that people who apply high-concentration DEET over long periods of time have a higher incidence of certain neurological disorders. I should emphasize that these disorders are usually associated with extremely high use. However, because the effects seem real, the current recommendation is to limit the concentration of DEET to 30% for adults and 10% in products used on kids less than 12 years old, and *not to use DEET at all on infants less than 2 months old*.

After 50 years during which DEET was the only really effective insect repellent, a new contender has recently entered the arena. **Picaridin**, also called icaridin, is a colorless and odorless liquid that matches the effectiveness of DEET but is less irritating and does not dissolve plastics or damage synthetic fabrics. Picaridin is currently (2008) available in a number of insect-repellent products.

What about skin-care lotions that some people say work? In recent years the skin-care lotion *Avon Skin So Soft*™ has been touted as an effective alternative by people who are concerned about using DEET-based repellents. The manufacturer does not claim insect-repellent effects for their product, but plenty of users do. In scientific trials *Skin So Soft*™ proved to be somewhat effective, but it does not provide long-lasting protection. It has to be reapplied frequently and does not prevent bites when pest numbers are high. In fact, any strong-smelling lotion is likely to mask some of the odors that insects use to find us. The effect will be temporary, however. With the recent introduction of much more effective DEET alternatives like picaridin, which is a true repellent, I suspect that the use of skin-care products as alternatives to true insect-repellents will decline.

site/default.asp) to manage populations of mosquitoes, black flies, and other public health pests on a regional basis. Homeowners, however, are largely limited to (1) avoiding areas of known infestation and (2) using **insect repellents**. The effectiveness of most repellents is somewhat uneven for black flies, however—sometimes they work, but sometimes they don't. If black flies are a severe nuisance where you live, the best approach may be to work with your local government to establish a regional black fly, or vector, control program.

Internet resources:

www.livingwithbugs.com/black_fly.html (black flies)
www.livingwithbugs.com/mos_repe.html (repellents)

Fleas (Siphonaptera)

The role of fleas in natural ecosystems: Adult fleas are ectoparasites of warm-blooded animals, while flea larvae are scavengers in the host's nest.

Most people know what fleas on cats and dogs look like. If you have not looked closely, however, you may not have noticed that fleas are flattened side-to-side. This shape allows them to move easily between hairs. Fleas have no wings but are able to jump to escape danger. Flea larvae are another matter; they look

Left: **biting flea**. Head of flea is to the left. Reproduced in color on Plate 1. Modified from Ken Gray Collection, courtesy of Oregon State University (# G176-13). Right: **flea larva**. This stage does not bite and is dependent on adult fleas for food. Modified from Ken Gray Collection, courtesy of Oregon State University (# 270-13). Reproduced in color on Plate 1.

nothing like the adults and don't live on the host animal. Flea larvae are small, white worms that live in the bedding or nest of the host animal. Flea larvae don't bite to obtain a meal of blood, like adult fleas do, but rather depend on dry blood defecated by the adults (this is usually where non-entomologists stop reading). This dry blood is sometimes called flea dirt.

Dried blood or **flea dirt** found in an animal's coat is a sure sign of a flea infestation. This debris is often uncovered during combing. Flea dirt will dissolve in water and turn the water blood red and can thus be distinguished from ordinary dirt. Excessive scratching or biting is another possible sign of fleas. Fleas can remain in a vacant building for months, even up to a year. It is fairly common for a house or apartment that has been vacant for months to unleash a flea infestation when new residents move

Fleas and human history

Despite their small size, fleas have had a profound effect on human history. Certain fleas can harbor a pathogenic bacterium in their gut that causes a deadly disease called **bubonic plague**, or bubonic fever. This disease spreads rapidly in crowded urban populations that are exposed to infected fleas, usually rat fleas. The mortality rate is high and death can occur quickly.

Throughout history there have been at least three pandemics of bubonic plague. The worst, between 1349 and about 1352, killed roughly 25% of the population of Europe. The bacterium was carried to Europe from central Asia on shipboard rats and fleas. The 1349–1352 pandemic was the Great Mortality, or **Black Death**, of the Middle Ages (google "Black Death" for more information). Historians believe that this catastrophic event may actually have led to the European Renaissance, roughly a hundred years later, by forcing the surviving early Europeans to develop a more efficient, science-based society because the labor force had been so depleted by the plague. Even today, the bubonic plague bacterium can be found in fleas associated with rodents in various parts of the world, *including the western US.*

Invention of flea collar technology

Flea collars were introduced in 1964 as an effective and relatively safe way to protect pet dogs and cats from fleas. Flea collars are made from a special plastic that slowly releases flea-killing insecticide. The invention of the technology of **slow-release pesticides** is usually credited to Dr. Robert Goulding, Jr. His research was conducted in a small off-campus lab at Oregon State University. Dr. Goulding was a member of the Entomology Department at OSU (the department was closed in 2003) until his retirement in 1981. Dr. Goulding died in 1991.

in, with or without pets. The fleas emerge from dormant pupae that have lain in wait for months until potential host animals, including humans, are detected.

Fleas were once the bane of every pet owner, and pet owners had limited options for safe flea control. Area sprays and aerosol "bombs" of insecticide were never very effective, because much of a flea's adult life is spent on the animal, protected from these applications. **Flea collars** became popular in the 1970s and are still in use today; they are made from a special plastic that slowly releases insecticide over the animal's coat. Flea collars, however, are less effective the further away from the collar the fleas are located, so infestations around the animal's hindquarters are not well controlled, especially in larger animals. Ironically, flea collars may work a little better for ticks (see later this chapter) because these ectoparasites tend to attach around the animal's head closer to the collar. Another problem with flea collars is that they can cause a type of skin irritation called flea-collar dermatitis.

Nowadays, topically applied and oral flea medications (insecticides) have largely replaced flea collars. Topically applied medications are oily liquids that are applied directly to the animal's skin where they spread in the oily secretions to cover the whole body. Topically applied medications do not readily enter the bloodstream and are therefore less likely to have side effects.

Flea control in homes

If you want to control an existing infestation of fleas in your home, keep the following points in mind: remember that immature fleas live in the animal's nest and adult fleas live mostly on the animal, so *both places need to be treated.* First, thoroughly clean areas where your pet sleeps or spends significant amounts of time, such as the pet's bedding, a favorite rug, or an outdoor kennel. Launder bedding if possible. Once clean, treat these areas with a spray insecticide that contains the insect growth regulator **methoprene** (sometimes called Precor™). Next, treat your pets with one of the topically applied flea medications, such as Frontline™ or Advantage™. Be sure to observe the precautions for these medications, because some animals cannot tolerate them. Reapply the topical medications if fleas are again found during regular grooming. There is no need to treat the lawn for fleas, since neither adult fleas nor larvae live in your lawn.

However, some animals are highly sensitive to these compounds, so be cautious when first using them and watch for adverse reactions. Popular topically applied flea medications (in 2008) are Frontline™, Advantage™, and Bio Spot™. Bio Spot for dogs contains the insecticide **permethrin** which is *highly toxic to cats.* In fact, permethrin should not be used at all in households with cats. Oral medications or pills are also available that place the insecticide in the blood, so that fleas ingest it when they bite.

Internet resources:

www.livingwithbugs.com/fleas.html
www.en.wikipedia.org/wiki/Flea
www.en.wikipedia.org/wiki/Bubonic_plague
www.cdc.gov/ncidod/dvbid/plague/index.htm

Human lice (Anoplura)

The role of lice in natural ecosystems: All lice are ectoparasites of warm-blooded animals, where they feed on blood.

There are three species of lice that are ectoparasites of humans. Each species prefers a very distinct part of the body and can usually be identified by where it is found. **Head lice** (*Pediculus humanus capitis*) infest the head and scalp, whereas **body lice** (*Pediculus humanus corporis*) are found in clothing from which they move to the skin to feed. **Pubic lice** (*Phthirus pubis*, also called crab lice, or "crabs") infest the groin area or other regions of the body where relatively coarse hair grows.

Lice are small, wingless insects that have adapted to living on their warm-blooded hosts. Head and body lice, which may or may not be the same species, are about ¹⁄₁₆" long, usually pale in

Right: **head louse** (~ 2 mm = ¹⁄₁₀", rule marks = 1 mm). This louse was combed from hair and placed in a preservative (alcohol) for study. The preservative darkened the specimen which when alive was light tan in color. Reproduced in color on Plate 2. Below right: **pubic (crab) louse**. The overall body shape resembles that of a crab, which accounts for the vernacular name for a pubic lice infestation—crabs. This specimen is grasping a hair with its large claws. The red color at the tip of the abdomen is recently consumed blood that is being excreted. Reproduced in color on Plate 2. Modified from Ken Gray Collection, courtesy of Oregon State University (# 627-35). Below: **body lice eggs**. Eggs are laid in clothing; adult body lice closely resemble head lice. Modified from Ken Gray Collection, courtesy of Oregon State University (#524-26).

Parasites

A parasite is an organism that lives off another organism, which is called the **host**. For example, when a mosquito bites us the mosquito is the parasite and we are its host. Some parasites live on the outside of the host, feeding on blood they get by biting, and are called *ecto*parasites; while others—certain parasitic worms, for example—live internally and are called *endo*parasites.

color, and somewhat flattened. Head lice attach their tiny eggs directly to hairs, while body lice lay their eggs in the clothing of an infested individual. Lice move slowly and infestations develop over time, so that by the time a full-blown outbreak is detected it may have been going on for weeks or even longer.

Pubic lice look very different from either body lice or head lice. With their enlarged front claws, they look like tiny crabs in overall body shape. Pubic lice behave more like head lice, however, in that they remain on the host and lay eggs attached to body hairs. Public lice prefer coarser hair, and so tend to be found in the groin, armpits, and even eyelashes.

No louse (louse is the singular form of lice) survives for long away from its host, because it requires the warmth and moist

Grooming in great apes (chimpanzees, gorillas, orangutans)

If you have ever watched a group of chimpanzees at the zoo, you probably noticed them grooming by picking through each other's fur. The main purpose of this activity is to remove lice, lice nits, and other parasites. The lice that occur on chimps and gorillas (orangutans, for some reason, don't have lice) are different from human lice but are closely related. Interestingly, some scientists believe that this highly social nitpicking activity contributed to the development of other social behaviors in the primate line leading to humans.

DDT, body lice, and World War II

Body lice and epidemic typhus, a bacterial louse-borne disease, were rampant in Europe during World War II until the advent of the insecticide DDT. The stunning success of DDT in controlling lice, and stopping the epidemics, however, lead to widespread overuse of synthetic, man-made insecticides in agriculture and public health in the years following the war.

Many people thought that DDT and similar chemicals were a cure-all for any pest problem. It was not until the 1960s that we began to realize that indiscriminate use of these materials was damaging the environment and actually threatening human health. Rachel Carson's 1962 book *Silent Spring* (still in print) is credited with starting a movement to reduce the indiscriminate use of pesticides that eventually led to the creation of the Environmental Protection Agency (EPA) in the US a decade later.

conditions found next to the host's skin. A louse infestation is called **pediculosis**, and medications that treat lice infestations are called **pediculocides**. Lice eggs are called **nits**; the term nitpicking refers to the practice of physically removing lice eggs from body hairs using special combs or simply the fingernails.

Head lice and pubic lice attach their eggs, or nits, to individual body hairs whereas body lice lay their eggs in clothing. All active stages of lice feed on blood that is obtained by biting the host. Louse bites result in red, itchy lesions. Chronic infestations of body lice result in dark, hardened areas of skin. Body lice can transmit the organism that causes **epidemic typhus** and some other diseases, but epidemics of these diseases are today generally confined to areas of natural disaster or civil conflict.

Head lice infestations in school-age children are very common and not confined to any particular region or socioeconomic group. Kids are susceptible to head lice because of the relatively thin skin of their scalp and the manner of their physical play, that is, close kid-to-kid contact. The first sign of infestation may be a note brought home from school, or possibly visible irritation and scratching at the back of the child's neck. *Don't panic*—head lice are manageable and there is *no risk from louse-borne disease.*

The key to head lice control is nit control, as any self-respecting chimp knows. If you eliminate nits the infestation can be managed, because the active lice stages can be simply washed out of the hair with medicated shampoo. If, on the other hand, nits are not eliminated, they will quickly hatch to replace the population of biting lice that were eliminated by other means. Nit control is best accomplished by hand-picking nits, which is slow

No-nit policies in schools

In response to pressure from parents, some schools have adopted a so-called no-nit policy when it comes to screening children for head lice. These policies generally state that if nits (lice eggs) or lice are found on a child, she will not be allowed to attend school until the infestation is eliminated. Are no-nit policies effective? Probably not. Do they cause unnecessary lost school days? Yes. While I support and empathize with schools in their desire to mange head lice, I think there are better ways.

The main problem with these policies is the risk of what's called a false positive. It is very difficult to tell the difference between live lice eggs (nits) and dead eggs, or eggs that have already hatched. Likewise, it is sometimes difficult to tell the difference between lice eggs and dandruff or other debris found in kid's hair. A false positive occurs when something other than a live nit is mistakenly identified as a live nit and the child is excluded from class.

I believe a better approach is for schools to develop a clear set of written guidelines regarding head lice treatment and prevention. The guidelines should be sent to parents each year at the beginning of school in the fall, and again if an outbreak occurs in a classroom. If there are enough resources, infested children who are not being treated at home could be treated at school instead. I think it is **important not to overly stigmatize individual children by identifying them publicly.** After all, head lice are not a health threat, since there are no diseases spread by these insects.

A parent's guide to head lice control

Parents often first become aware of their child's head lice when the child comes home from school with a note. *Don't panic.* There are proven ways to deal with the infestation safely, and since head lice do not carry diseases, the only real threat is the itching and skin irritation they cause. You'll need a good metal **nit comb**, a good **light source**, and a **medicated lice shampoo or creme rinse** (see the Internet resources below for where to obtain these supplies). You may also want one of the nit-combing aids that make nitpicking easier.

Apply the nit-combing aids or just a non-medicated creme rinse as directed, or simply wash your child's hair. Now for the hard part, for you and your child: with a strong light directed at her head, carefully comb the hair with a *metal* nit comb, starting at the scalp and working out. Comb a small amount of hair at a time, and take it slowly. The whole procedure could take an hour or more. The metal comb will remove lice and crush any nits that are attached to the hair shafts. Any lice that you find on the comb can be dropped into soapy water. If you do this nitpicking carefully enough, the infestation may be eliminated by this treatment alone, because you will remove all lice and eggs.

However, most of the time you won't be 100% effective at removing lice and eggs and some will remain to keep the infestation going. This is where the medicated lice shampoo and creme rinses come into the picture. Once the nitpicking is done as well as you can do it, or for as long as the child will sit still, apply a medicated lice shampoo or creme rinse product according to the package instructions. This treatment will kill the last of the infestation.

You are almost done. Next, wash bedding, washable clothing, and fabric-covered toys, etc. Cloth-covered articles that cannot be washed should be placed in a plastic bag and put in the freezer for a day or two. A chest-type freezer works great for large articles. This freezer treatment will kill all stages of lice. Don't get carried away with treating the house, furniture, or bedding, since lice do not live for long away from the host and so will not infest the house in general. *There is no need to treat the house or furnishings with insecticide.* ➤

> ➤ Finally, since a head lice infestation can sometimes be present for months before it is detected, you should check the hair and scalp of everyone in the household if a child is found with an active infestation. Anyone in the family that has lice or nits in their hair must be treated as well.

and laborious, or by the use of special fine-tooth lice combs—a slightly less labor-intensive method. Either way, it does no good to eliminate active lice if you leave behind healthy lice eggs.

Body lice look like head lice but behave very differently. Body lice are content to spend most of their lives in the host's clothing and only venture to the host's skin to feed. They even lay their eggs in clothing rather than attached to hairs, as head lice and pubic lice do. Since body lice live on and lay eggs in clothing, they are more easily managed by regular laundering of clothes and good personal hygiene, where this is possible. Because clothing care is so critical to body lice control, these ectoparasites are generally only a problem today when clothes are not regularly washed, such as in homeless or displaced populations and during natural disasters.

Pubic lice are controlled in the same manner as head lice—with nitpicking and medicated shampoos or lotions. Since pubic lice infestation is often considered to be a sexually transmitted condition, because of the usual location of the infestation, partners of infested individuals should be treated as well. **Pubic lice do not carry sexually transmitted diseases**, however.

Internet resources:

www.livingwithbugs.com/headlice.html
www.livingwithbugs.com/pubic_lice.html
www.livingwithbugs.com/body_lice.html
www.en.wikipedia.org/wiki/Pediculosis

Biting midges (Ceratopogonidae)

The role of biting midges in natural ecosystems: Adult midges are ectoparasites of warm-blooded animals. Midge larvae are predators and scavengers that live in damp soil.

Biting midges are tiny (1–2 mm or about ⅟₁₆") gnat-like biting flies that are closely related to mosquitoes and sometimes called no-see-ums or punkies. Like mosquitoes, female biting midges bite to obtain blood. Bites can be painful and sometimes result in an allergic reaction in both humans and livestock. **Sweet itch** is an allergic condition in horses resulting from the bite of these insects. Biting midges are so small that people sometimes report being bitten but *not seeing what bit them at all*. These insects are often described as *vicious, daytime biters*, in contrast to mosquitoes which often bite in the evening. Biting midges can significantly impact tourist activity, especially near coastal areas all over the world.

Biting midge larvae are aquatic or semi-aquatic organisms that live in damp soil or leaf litter; they are therefore common in areas of wet soils, poorly drained pastures, and marshes. Biting midges have been associated with disease transmission in both people and livestock throughout the world, but it is the irritation caused by their bites that generally gets the most attention.

Control of adult or larval midges is very difficult and not usually attempted by homeowners, but there are a few things you can do to lessen the annoyance caused by these pests. Firstly, try to avoid areas of known infestation. Biting midges tend to be spotty and somewhat confined to areas of poorly drained soil, where their larvae develop. Any measure that improves drainage in fields and pastures will likely reduce the ability of biting midges to breed. Biting midges can even be found in the residential landscape if soils are allowed to remain too wet. Secondly, insect repellents—especially those that contain **DEET** (N, N-diethyl-m-toluamide) or the newest repellent **picaridin** (icaridin)—are somewhat effective in providing personal protection (see Insect Repellents earlier in this chapter).

Internet resources:

www.en.wikipedia.org/wiki/Ceratopogonidae
www.livingwithbugs.com/swe_itch.html
www.en.wikipedia.org/wiki/DEET
www.en.wikipedia.org/wiki/Icaridin

Mosquitoes (Culicidae)

The role of mosquitoes in natural ecosystems: Adult mosquitoes
are ectoparasites of warm-blooded animals. Mosquito larvae are
predators and scavengers that live in fresh or brackish water.

Almost everyone knows what an adult mosquito looks and
sounds like, but larval mosquitoes are less well known; unless you
know what you're looking for, they are difficult to find. Mosquito
larvae live in still water, in contrast to black fly larvae which require
fresh flowing water. Some mosquitoes prefer fresh water, but other
species prefer the brackish, or slightly salty, water that is found
near the ocean. Mosquito larvae feed on other aquatic organisms
and are restricted to relatively clean water. In fact, scientists sometimes use aquatic organisms like mosquito and black fly larvae to
measure the relative purity of streams, lakes, and ponds.

Mosquito larvae are worm-like wrigglers that often hang upside down in the water. Some larvae breathe through gills while

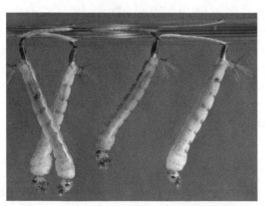

Mosquito larvae suspended
head down in water. Modified
from Ken Gray Collection,
courtesy of Oregon State
University (# 295-32).

Malaria and the West Nile virus

The list of mosquito-borne human diseases is long and woven throughout human history. One ancient and one modern disease, however, serve to illustrate the range of impacts that mosquitoes have, beyond their annoying, itchy bites. **Malaria** is an often fatal parasitic disease that infects the blood and major organs of the body; it has been around since the beginning of recorded history. **West Nile virus**, on the other hand, has only recently been recognized as important, and while it is sometimes serious, it does not pose the threat that malaria does.

Because mosquitoes inject a small amount of saliva each time they bite, the area around the bite usually swells and becomes itchy. This reaction is caused by our body's defenses against the foreign proteins in the mosquito saliva. This saliva may also contain disease-causing organisms.

Malaria is a disease that infects hundreds of millions of people annually and still *kills 1 to 3 million people worldwide each year*. It is caused by a microbe that is transmitted by certain mosquitoes when they bite. Nowadays malaria is mostly confined to the tropical regions of the world, but it was once more widespread. In fact, the name malaria comes form the Italian words for "bad air," *mala aria*. Medieval Italians thought that it was foul-smelling air emanating from the swamps surrounding Rome that caused the disease. We now know that it was the mosquitoes breeding in the still waters of the swamps that caused the malarial fever.

West Nile virus is a disease mainly in birds; humans are only secondary or accidental hosts. The virus causes death in birds but generally only mild flu-like symptoms in humans. More serious conditions may develop in a small percentage of cases, however. In the US roughly 100 to 300 deaths occur each year from West Nile virus.

others use a snorkel-like airway to the water surface. One way to control mosquitoes is to apply a thin oil film to the water surface that clogs these breathing tubes. Mosquitoes lay their eggs in or near the water in which the larvae develop. Mosquitoes can develop from eggs to adults in only a few weeks under some conditions, so even small, temporary rain puddles or any water-filled containers provide suitable breeding grounds. Landscape fountains, ponds, planters, gutters, bird baths, etc. can all serve as a breeding source for mosquitoes.

Female mosquitoes must find blood in order to lay healthy eggs. Male mosquitoes do not bite and are rarely even seen. Females use their senses of smell and sight to find a suitable host. They first locate an object that seems to be about the right size and shape; then they fly closer and actually use smell to home in on a feeding site. The exact chemical signals that mosquitoes use to locate us at close range are complex and not completely understood. However, scientists have discovered that insect repellents actually interfere with these chemical cues and make us invisible to mosquitoes and other blood-feeding critters (see Insect Repellents earlier in this chapter).

You might not want to think about it, but when a mosquito bites it actually injects the wound with a little of its saliva in order to help the blood flow more easily. This saliva may contain a variety of disease-causing microorganisms such as viruses and bacteria, along with the anti-coagulant chemicals that keep blood flowing. Once injected, the microbes and viruses can multiply and cause diseases such as malaria, yellow fever, and—most recently in the news—West Nile virus. Because of their ability to infect humans with deadly diseases, mosquitoes have always been, and continue to be, very important in shaping human history and influencing where people live.

Mosquito control around homes begins with **water management**. Since mosquitoes need water to breed, the fewer sources of fresh water—yard ornaments, clogged gutters, untreated landscape ponds, and pools of standing water resulting from overwatering or a leaky irrigation system—the better. One mosquito species, for example, is known to specialize in breeding in the water that accumulates in discarded automobile tires. Another species specializes in using the water held in certain flowers called pitcher plants.

Sources of standing water on your property should be treated to prevent them from becoming sources of mosquitoes. The simplest treatment is to drain the water and allow the container to dry. The second best treatment is to flush the container with a strong stream of water at least once a week during warm months of the year. This method works well for small fountains and bird baths, for example. Small water features can also be treated with hot water alone to kill mosquito larvae, without using pesticides.

The most important thing that you can do to protect yourself from bites is to use an insect repellent when mosquitoes are around and bites are possible. Insect repellents that contain the chemical DEET (*N*,*N*-diethyl-*m*-toluamide) are still the most effective overall, but there are a variety of new products on the market that offer some alternatives (see section about Insect Repellents earlier in this chapter).

Use of insect or **mosquito netting** is another way to avoid bites from mosquitoes and black flies. This fine mesh netting can be made into large tent-like nets that cover beds, or small nets that hang from hat brims and protect the head and neck. Bed nets alone are very effective for preventing malaria and other diseases

Bacillus thuringiensis israelensis (*Bti*)

This is the scientific name for a natural soil bacterium that makes a protein that is highly toxic to mosquito larvae and other closely related insects (such as black flies and biting midges), but is practically non-toxic to everything else. This selectiveness makes *Bti* an almost prefect pesticide for these pests. It can be safely used in ponds or natural streams with fish and other aquatic organisms. *Bti* is commercially produced by fermentation and is widely used for mosquito control in a large number of different products. Homeowners can purchase *Bti* in molded cakes called dunks, or as granules. *Bti*, in whatever form, is placed in standing water, where it slowly dissolves and releases the toxic protein. Since mosquito larvae filter water in order to feed on tiny aquatic organisms they are exposed to the toxic protein and die.

Municipal vector control

Cities or other governmental entities often set up regional control programs for specific pests, especially pests like mosquitoes that are carriers of disease. For example, your county may have a program for managing populations of mosquitoes or other biting pests. Without you even knowing about it, there may be efforts to manage these pests on your behalf. These programs are often organized into entities called vector control districts. A vector is an organism that can pass disease-causing microbes and viruses from one animal to another. Contact your city or county government and see what vector control is going on in your neighborhood. If you have a problem with mosquitoes or some other biting pest, you may even be able to goad local officials into starting a control district if one does not already exist.

that are carried by those mosquitoes that bite mainly at night.

Internet resources:

www.livingwithbugs.com/mosquit.html
www.livingwithbugs.com/malaria.html
www.en.wikipedia.org/wiki/Malaria
www.cdc.gov/ncidod/dvbid/westnile/index.htm

Ticks (Ixodidae and Argasidae)

The role of ticks in natural ecosystems: Ticks are ectoparasites of vertebrate animals such as reptiles and mammals.

If you are a dog owner and your pet spends much time outdoors, you probably know what a tick looks like. Dogs are tick magnets and will pick up these blood-sucking arthropods as they run through brushy areas and explore animal burrows where ticks like to hang out. For this reason, ticks are often found around the head and neck areas. Most people are familiar with ticks on their pets, but people and other **vertebrate** animals get ticks as well. Since ticks, like other blood-feeding arthropods, may carry a variety of blood-borne diseases, we need to protect ourselves as well as our pets.

Ticks are small to medium-sized arthropods that generally have eight legs and are more closely related to mites and spiders than to insects. All active stages are **ectoparasites** of mammals, birds, and reptiles (see *Parasites* earlier in this chapter). The term ectoparasite means that ticks feed on the outside (the *ecto* part) and bite to withdraw blood (the *parasite* part). Blood is a tick's only source of food and water. When ticks feed, their bodies expand to a condition called engorged.

Ticks can be found in any brushy, wooded, or weedy area.

Above: **spinose ear tick** (~0.37"), a type of soft tick. Notice that the head of this soft tick is *not visible* from above (compare to picture of American dog tick, a hard tick, in which the head is visible from above). Reproduced in color on Plate 3. Modified from Ken Gray Collection, courtesy of Oregon State University (#174-8). Above right: **unfed hard tick** (*Dermacentor albipictus*) (~0.18"). Reproduced in color on Plate 3. Modified from Ken Gray Collection, courtesy of Oregon State University (#259-15). Right: **fed (engorged) hard tick**, probably American dog tick (about ¼" long). This tick had completed feeding and was in the process of detaching from our dog when it was found. Engorged hard ticks can sometimes be mistaken for soft ticks. Reproduced in color on Plate 3. Photo by J. D. DeAngelis.

Since ticks infest mainly wild animals such as deer and small rodents, ticks will be more numerous in habitats that support these animals. Certain ticks are also found in animal burrows.

Ticks feed by inserting their mouthparts through the skin and withdrawing blood. Some ticks may glue themselves to the skin surface of their host while feeding, which makes removing them difficult. Unlike other blood-feeding critters like mosquitoes and black flies, ticks can remain attached to their hosts for *many hours or even days* while feeding. There is good evidence that the longer ticks are attached, the greater the chance that disease organisms will be passed from tick to host. In fact, some studies have shown that when ticks are removed within 24 hours, the chance for disease transmission is small or even zero.

You should *not* try to control ticks in your yard with insecticides. It would be a waste of time and money trying to identify

Lyme disease

Lyme disease is a serious blood disorder transmitted by the bite of certain ticks. The disease is caused by a microorganism in the saliva that enters the wound when ticks bite. Two species of ticks in North America are primarily responsible for the transmission of Lyme disease, one in the mid-west and eastern states (*Ixodes scapularis*) and a different species in western states (*Ixodes pacificus*).

When I worked in North Carolina, one of the county Extension offices reported that a client had come in to their Insect Identification Clinic with a large tick attached to his neck that he said had been there for *three days!* The client said that he didn't know how to remove it safely, so he figured it was better to just leave it alone. This is absolutely wrong. Ticks should be removed as quickly as possible, because the chance that disease will be passed from tick to human increases dramatically the longer a tick is allowed to feed.

Lyme disease is the most common tick-borne infection in both North America and Europe, but ticks carry other serious diseases as well. The bottom line is that *ticks should be removed from you and your pets as soon as they are discovered.*

How to safely remove ticks

The easiest and safest way to remove a tick is to grab it by the mouthparts (the organs used for feeding) and pull straight up and out. Use a loop of strong sewing thread or fishing line to lasso the mouthparts by passing the loop over the back of the tick and pulling on the ends of the line until the tick pops off. A stiff fishing line works better. You can also use tweezers to snag the mouthparts, but be careful not to stab your patient with the pointed end. Don't worry if the mouthparts break off in the wound; at worst they will cause a minor secondary infection. Finally, clean the wound and apply an over-the-counter antibiotic.

Be very careful not to squeeze the tick's body while removing it, because this may actually force disease organisms into the wound. Also, don't put anything *on* the tick in an effort to smother it and force the tick to let go. The fact is that when ticks bite, they may seal their mouthparts onto the wound and they are then unable to back away until feeding is complete.

the few places in your yard where ticks are likely to be, and you would end up having to live with all the pesticide you applied. Instead, practice good preventative measures. Check yourself and your pets whenever you return from outdoor activities that take you into areas where ticks are common. These include bushy areas and areas where nests of rodents and small animals (mice, voles, rabbits, etc.) are abundant. Apply insect repellents to yourself and treat your pets with one of the flea-control medications that also controls ticks. **Flea collars** are also somewhat effective for protection against ticks, although, ironically, they are not particularly effective against fleas. *Never use flea collars on people because they will cause skin burns.*

Internet resources:

www.livingwithbugs.com/tick_spi.html
www.en.wikipedia.org/wiki/lyme_disease
www.cdc.gov/ncidod/dvbid/lyme/index.htm

Chapter 2
Insects that damage building materials

Fortunately there are relatively few insects that actually damage wood and/or other types of building materials (Table 1), and the damage caused by many of these is really pretty minimal. There are some, however, that can cause significant and costly damage and these insects are the subjects of this chapter. Everyone knows at least a little about **termites**, but there are a few other insects that can be equally damaging under certain circumstances. In the US, termites probably account for more damage overall than any other structural pest, but in some areas **carpenter ants** actually outstrip termites in terms of their potential for damage. Apart from termites and carpenter ants, the only other true structural pests are two different families of **powderpost beetles**. Refer to Table 1 (on pages 48 and 49) as we discuss these and other structural pests in the pages that follow.

Carpenter ants (*Camponotus spp.*)

The role of carpenter ants in natural ecosystems: Carpenter ants, like other ants, are predators and scavengers. Carpenter ants forage for all sorts of food, including plant nectar, aphid honeydew, animal carrion, other insects, and seeds.

Imagine that you've recently noticed a soft, springy spot in your kitchen floor. You immediately assume that a water leak from the nearby dishwasher has led to a rotted subfloor so you

Carpenter ants. The large ant (left, about ½" long) is a **worker** that gathers food and builds and defends the nest. The winged ant (right, about ½–⅝" long) is a **queen**, responsible for starting new colonies and laying all the eggs. Reproduced in color on Plate 4. Modified from Ken Gray Collection, courtesy of Oregon State University (#193-20 and #193-18).

call in a carpenter to have a look. After removing the floor covering, the carpenter has some good news and some bad news. The good news is that you don't have a water leak, the bad news is that you have a huge carpenter ant nest that has damaged the floor joists, subflooring, and insulation. Total repair estimate is $15,000! This is a largely true story, and it is not uncommon for carpenter ant damage to be discovered in this way during repair work or remodeling. If the homeowners had done an **annual inspection for structural pests** they might have detected ant activity years earlier and been able to prevent this damage.

Most ants are small and nest underground, only rarely becoming anything more than a nuisance (see chapter 4). **Carpenter ants**, on the other hand, are large, powerful ants that nest above ground in cavities such as tree stumps and sometimes in the walls, subfloors, or roofs of our houses. Carpenter ants are large, black

Structural pests

The term *structural pest* means different things to different people. Some entomologists (people who study insects and related arthropods), use the term to include insects that infest stored grains, foodstuff, and building materials, while others restrict the term to insects that only infest and/or damage wood and other building materials. I prefer the second, more restrictive, definition.

Table 1: Wood-Damaging Insects

name	identification	types of damage
Carpenter ants	Large black or reddish-black ants that nest in cavities above ground	Nests constructed in solid material. Damage occurs when nests are expanded
Termites	Delicate insects that construct colonies in wood	Termites consume wood fiber (cellulose); damage usually starts on the inside
Lyctid powderpost beetles	Small, reddish-brown to black beetles. Head visible from above	Beetle larvae bore into and destroy wood; larvae feed on starch
Anobiid powderpost beetles	Small, reddish-brown to black beetles. Head not visible from above	Beetle larvae bore into and destroy wood; larvae feed on starch
Round-headed wood borers	Sometimes large, cream-colored wood-boring larvae with distinct head capsule. Adults often large, colorful beetles with long antennae	Beetle larvae bore in living or recently dead trees or wood that is less than 10 years old; large tunnels
Flat-headed wood borers	Adult beetles often with metallic coloration. Wood-boring larvae sometimes with flattened region behind head	Beetle larvae bore in living or recently dead trees; large tunnels
Horntail wood wasps	Large, wasp-like insects with a long, harmless "stinger." Wasps may emerge in newly constructed homes (up to 3 years old)	Little structural damage; damage is limited to aesthetic damage to wall and floor coverings
Carpenter bees	Large, heavy-bodied bees that resemble bumble bees.	Large entrance hole with tunnels usually at right angles to entrance, allowing water and rot fungi to enter

Adapted from H. B. Moore (1979), Wood-Inhabiting Insects in Houses: Their Identification, Biology, Prevention and Control. USDA, FS, DHUD publication

damage sites	exit holes?	how damaging?
Structural softwoods, soft building materials such as insulation board	No emergence holes per se; ants enter and exit colony to forage for food and water	Can be extremely damaging if left untreated for years
Generally softwoods, but sometimes hardwoods, too	Termites generally remain in the infested wood; mud shelter tubes indicate an active infestation	Can be extremely damaging, especially in warm or tropical climates
Mostly hardwoods: furniture, flooring, cabinets	Small, round holes about $1/16$" in diameter; very fine, dusty powder	Can cause extensive cosmetic damage; occasionally cause internal damage
Mostly structural softwoods; especially damaging in damp climates	Small, circular holes about the size of a pencil lead; fine or gritty powder	Can cause extensive structural damage if not treated
Hardwoods and softwoods	Large (¼"–½"), circular to oval	Damage is limited, because these beetles do not normally reinfest wood after the first generation. The old house borer may sometimes reinfest
Hardwoods and softwoods	Large (¼"–½"), flattened to oval holes	Damage is generally limited to first generation
Wasps emerge from softwoods used as structural components of walls and floors	Large (½"), round holes that often appear in interior wall surfaces such as wallboard.	Damage is generally limited to the initial exit holes because these wasps do not reinfest
Exterior trim wood, doors, siding, etc.	Large, round holes	Damage is minimal, but holes should be treated and repaired to prevent water infiltration

Damage to a subfloor caused by carpenter ants. This damage was caused by a large carpenter ant nest that had been constructed between the floor joists, under the insulation. The wood shown is a piece of the subflooring. Notice how the ants have removed the softer rings and left the hard growth rings. The colony was discovered because the floor had become soft and springy. Photo by J. D. DeAngelis.

ants, sometimes with dark brown or dark red areas. All carpenter ants belong to the large and diverse genus *Camponotus*. The reproductive, winged, stage can be as large as ¾" (20 mm) long, while workers are generally ¼" (6.5 mm)–½" (13 mm) in length.

Damage to our homes and other structures occurs when these powerful ants excavate and enlarge their cavity nests to make room for a growing colony. Unlike termites, another important structural insect pest, carpenter ants do not eat wood. They forage outside the colony for food and water and this is the key to detecting their activity during routine inspections.

Like other ants, carpenter ants live in colonies that are started by a queen. Mated queens generally fly during late spring and locate a suitable cavity in which to begin laying eggs. A queen can use almost any protected cavity, such as inside a wall, under floor insulation, or outside in a tree stump. The cavity is not always associated with wood, since carpenter ants do not necessarily need wood for survival, unlike termites. For example, rigid foam insulation is frequently damaged by these ants. Carpenter ant colonies can exist for many years, growing and expanding their damage.

In the eastern US, ant damage is often associated with moisture, because colonies tend to start where wood has been moisture-damaged; this is not necessarily the case in the western US, where colonies and damage can occur in very dry situations.

Once a batch of worker ants—the ants that enlarge the nest and forage for food—has been reared by the queen, she stays within the nest for the remainder of her life. Workers are the ones that leave the nest to search for food and water. Carpenter ants are opportunistic predators and scavengers, and take a wide variety of foods. This behavior of moving between nest and foraging grounds, combined with their large size, makes carpenter ant activity within a building relatively easy to detect if you look in the right place. You'll sometimes see ants trailing (moving in single file) between the structure and outdoors as they forage outside for food and water.

As carpenter ant colonies grow, worker ants excavate whatever is around the nest to enlarge the original cavity. It is this **colony expansion** activity that causes damage to building materials. Colonies can continue to grow over many years and may split into several satellite colonies when the original colony grows too large.

If you detect carpenter ant activity suggesting that a nest, or nests, may be present in your home and decide that control is needed, it may be wise to call in a pest-control company to do the work (see chapter 12). This is one of the few pest-control jobs that most homeowners will not want to do themselves. Standard, conventional treatments to control carpenter ants involve creating a barrier of insecticide inside the walls of your home that ants must cross in order to forage for food and water. This involves drilling into walls—something most homeowners will not want to tackle. If you decide to let a pest-control company treat for carpenter ants, take a look at chapter 12 (Buying pest-control services) for some suggestions.

If you are the do-it-yourself type, new methods of carpenter ant treatment offer some hope that homeowners can tackle this pest by themselves. As of 2008, there is now one insecticide registered as a **perimeter treatment** for carpenter ants that is so effective it may replace drilling wall voids as a standard treatment. The perimeter treatment can be combined with carpenter-ant baits which are another new addition to the control arsenal. Baits can be used in areas where conventional insecticides cannot, or

Inspecting your home for structural pests

All homeowners should inspect their home for the three most common structural insect pests *at least once a year*. If you don't want do it yourself, you can hire a pest control company to do it for you. The basic inspection is pretty simple and should take only about an hour.

Start by taking a walk around the exterior of your home on a warm summer morning or evening, when carpenter ants should be active. Ants won't be active enough when it is too cold or too hot. Make note of any plants that touch the house, either foundation plantings or just bushes that have grown too big over the years. Plan to remove or cut back this vegetation so there is at least an 18" gap between plants and the house. Carpenter ants will use vegetation that touches the house as a bridge to avoid certain methods of control. Vegetation along the foundation also hides these surfaces and makes inspecting more difficult. *Don't forget the roof.* Remove any vegetation that touches the roof such as overhanging tree limbs. As you walk, inspect the lower foundation and siding and look for large ants that seem to be trailing from the house out into the yard or back into the house. If you find ants collect a few in a jar with a cotton ball soaked in alcohol and take them to your Cooperative Extension office (see Appendix) for identification.

The next two inspections are a little more difficult and depend on how much access you have to the underside of your home. Some homes, especially in the western US, are built over a crawl space, from which you can see the underside of the first floor and all the floor joists. Some homes are built over an enclosed basement or a combination of crawl space and basement. Still other homes are built on a slab of concrete with virtually no access to the underside of the first floor (see chapter 8).

If you have access to a crawl space, go in there with a good flashlight (yes, I know there are spiders in there). Look for **mud shelter tubes** (see Termites) reaching from the soil to the structural wood of the home. Inspect all foundation walls, sill plate, and posts that span the gap between soil and house. Shelter tubes should alert you to ➤

➤ a possible termite infestation. Finally, inspect posts and beams for the telltale holes and sawdust of anobiid powderpost beetles. The inspection for anobiid powderpost beetles is especially important for homes in relatively wet climates such as coastal areas.

These annual inspections will not, of course, guarantee that you'll never have damage from structural pests but they will go a long way toward protecting your most valuable asset. If you live in a tropical or semi-tropical climate, like the southeastern US or Hawaii, you should inspect your home at least *twice* a year for pests and water damage.

should not, be used, such as near water wells or indoors. See the online resources for updated information about new carpenter-ant treatments.

Internet resources:

www.livingwithbugs.com/carp_ant.html
www.livingwithbugs.com/inspect.html

Carpenter bees (*Xylocopa spp.*)

The role of carpenter bees in natural ecosystems: Carpenter bees feed on plant nectar and pollen, much like honey bees.

Carpenter bees are large, colorful bees that look somewhat like bumble bees. Carpenter bees occasionally construct nests in exterior structural or decorative wood such as siding, fascia

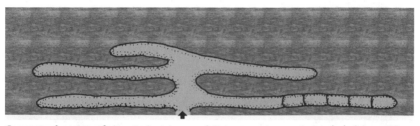

Carpenter bee tunnels in exterior trim wood. Bees excavate an entrance hole (arrow, ½" diameter) then turn and tunnel along the wood grain. (Drawing modified from H. B. Moore (1979), *Wood-Inhabiting Insects in Houses: Their Identification, Biology, Prevention and Control.* USDA, FS, DHUD publication)

boards, trim, and log homes. Bees chew a round ½" diameter hole in the wood surface then bore a tunnel, usually at 90 degrees to the entrance hole. The tunnels may be used year after year, and each year they are lengthened. Damage is caused by this repeated use of the wood which may eventually weaken it directly or allow water to penetrate, causing rot.

Unfinished wood surfaces are far more likely to be attacked by carpenter bees than finished wood. Paint works better than stain to resist carpenter bees, but stain is better than no finish at all. The bottom line is that the heavier the surface finish, the better the protection against this bee. Softer wood is generally selected and **surfaces in direct light**, as opposed to those in shadow, are preferred by these bees.

Carpenter bee holes should be repaired to prevent bees from enlarging tunnels year after year. If left open, the entrance holes may allow water and rot fungi to attack wood, which in the long run will cause more damage than the bees themselves. To repair carpenter bee damage you'll need some exterior caulk and an insecticide (see Internet resources below) to treat around the holes. Treat around the entrance holes at the approved rate using a garden sprayer, allow to dry for several days, then seal the hole with caulk or a wooden plug, and finish to match the existing surface.

Internet resources:

www.livingwithbugs.com/carpenter_bee.html

Horntail wood wasps (Siricidae)

The role of horntail wood wasps in natural ecosystems: Horntail larvae feed on the remains of dead trees and hasten the decomposition process.

These large insects lay their eggs in recently dead trees. They are common, for example, in standing dead trees killed by forest

Horntail wood wasp (~1.75"). These large but harmless wasps sometimes emerge from framing lumber in recently built homes. Note the large but harmless "stinger" extending from the tail end (left). Reproduced in color on Plate 4. Modified from Ken Gray Collection, courtesy of Oregon State University (# 379-22)

fires in the western US. The larvae tunnel in the dead wood, where they complete development in two to five years and emerge as fully grown wasps. New homeowners can encounter this insect because infested trees may be harvested and turned into framing lumber that is then used to build new homes. When the horntail wasps complete their development in the framing lumber they can emerge into homes. The wasps are harmless—they won't harm people and they won't reinfest the wood in the home—but they sure make a lot of noise and startle the unsuspecting new homeowners, who then immediately call their lawyer!

No control treatments are necessary. The only action that is needed is repair of the wall or floor covering where the wasp has chewed through the surface. Wasp activity can last up to 5 years following home construction, but is usually over in 3 years.

Internet resources:

www.en.wikipedia.org/wiki/Horntail

Powderpost beetles (Anobiidae and Lyctidae)

There are a number of beetles that use dead trees, or even milled lumber, to lay eggs and develop their young. Beetle larvae feed on starch reserves in the wood that were formed when the tree was alive. Most of these insects, however, cannot infest live trees because of the tree's natural defenses. The most common wood-boring beetles belong to just four families—the long-horned, or round-headed, wood borers (Cerambycidae), flat-headed, or metallic, wood borers (Buprestidae), anobiid powderpost beetles (Anobiidae) and the lyctid powderpost beetles (Lyctidae). With a few exceptions, the powderpost beetles are the only ones able to infest seasoned wood and sustain an infestation beyond the first generation and therefore do significant damage.

Powderpost beetles are small beetles that infest both hardwoods and softwoods. Despite their size, these beetles are capable of causing **extensive damage to wood** because they can reinfest seasoned wood. The female beetle lays her eggs on the wood surface. Tiny beetle larvae bore in through small cracks and larvae develop by consuming starch that is found in the wood cells. Extensive internal damage to wood can be done by the boring larvae. Larvae take months to years to complete development and adult beetles emerge through **circular emergence holes** on the wood surface. Beetles live only a short time, just long enough to mate and lay eggs for the next generation.

Wood may be infested even after it has been kiln-dried and milled into lumber. Infestation of milled wood occurs when dried wood is improperly stored near an active infestation. Kiln-drying alone does not confer protection against infestation but it does eliminate any larvae that were present at the time the wood entered the dryer.

There are two families of beetles commonly called powderpost

Softwoods versus hardwoods

Wood is classified as either softwood or hardwood based on the species of tree from which it was cut. Softwoods are cut from conifers (cone-bearing trees) such as pine, spruce, cedar, Douglas fir, hemlock, and redwood. Hardwoods are cut from broad-leaf trees such as oak, maple, cherry, ash, and hickory. Depending on the species, some softwoods are actually harder and stronger than some hardwoods. In home building, softwood lumber is used mainly for framing and decorative trim while hardwoods are used for flooring, cabinets, and furniture.

beetles because of the powdery material that accumulates at the opening of their emergence holes. One family, the anobiids (Anobiidae) are more common in softwoods like pine, fir, Douglas fir, and spruce, while the lyctids (Lyctidae) are more common in hardwoods like oak, maple, and hickory. If you have ever noticed small, round holes in the wooden handle of an ax, for example, these may have been emergence holes of lyctid powderpost beetles.

Anobiid powderpost beetles (Anobiidae)

The role of powderpost beetles in natural ecosystems: Beetle larvae feed on the remains of dead trees and hasten the decomposition process.

Anobiid powderpost beetles are potentially the most destructive beetle pests of **softwoods**. These small, wood-boring insects damage mainly softwoods like fir, pine, and Douglas fir. What makes these beetles so potentially damaging is their **ability to reinfest the same piece of wood for many generations**. In other words, beetles that emerge from a ponderosa pine log used in constructing a log home, for example, may lay eggs and start a new generation in the same logs from which they emerged, thus continuing the infestation and damage.

Protecting wood from powderpost beetles

The best way to protect wood from powderpost beetles is to stop larvae that have hatched from eggs laid on the wood surface from boring into the wood. Once larvae get below the wood surface they are very difficult to manage. Fortunately there is a relatively non-toxic natural insecticide that is used to treat wood for both powderpost beetles and rot fungi. The insecticide is **boric acid** in the form of a mineral salt called borate, or borax (see chapter 4). Borate insecticides are formulated as liquids, sometimes with other chemicals that aid penetration into the wood (see Internet resources below).

Above: emergence holes (¹⁄₁₆" diameter) in oak flooring and particles of boring dust made by **lyctid powderpost beetles**. Left: round emergence holes (¹⁄₁₆"–¹⁄₈" diameter) made by **anobiid powderpost beetles**. These holes may have particles of wood (boring dust) associated with them. The presence or absence of boring dust is an indication of how recently the hole was made. Photos by J. D. DeAngelis

Internet resources:

www.livingwithbugs.com/powder.html

Lyctid powderpost beetles (Lyctidae)

The role of powderpost beetles in natural ecosystems: Beetle larvae feed on the remains of dead trees and hasten the decomposition process.

Whereas anobiids attack mostly softwoods, lyctid powderpost beetles (Lyctiidae) are potentially the most destructive beetle pests of **seasoned hardwoods**. These small, wood-boring insects damage mainly hardwoods such as oak, maple, ash, and hickory. Like anobiids, what makes these beetles so potentially damaging is their **ability to reinfest the same wood for many generations**. In other words, beetles that emerge from a piece of flooring or furniture may lay eggs and start a new generation in the same wood, thus continuing the infestation and damage.

Internet resources:

www.livingwithbugs.com/floor_beetles.html

Termites (Isoptera)

The role of termites in natural ecosystems: Termites consume wood and hasten the decomposition, or recycling, of wood and similar materials made of cellulose.

Termites are one of the very few insects that can do **significant damage** to buildings and homes if not managed. The damage potential of termites, however, is not the same everywhere. Their potential for damage is much higher in **warm climates** then it is in cool climates. So, for example, homes in the southeastern US are subject to far more termite damage than homes in the northwestern US. However, except for Alaska, the potential for termite damage occurs, more or less, in all parts of the United States.

There are many different species of termites; they can be combined into groups according to where they live and the condition of the wood they inhabit. There are **dampwood termites** that colonize mainly wood that is continually damp and rotted. These termites are generally found where the climate allows for wood to be damp during much of the year, such as parts of the coastal Pacific Northwest. Dampwood termites are not usually

Left: **Subterranean termite shelter tube, or "mud tube"** (on laboratory glassware). These tubes are constructed whenever termite workers move outside the colony. The presence of shelter tubes on above-ground structures can be used to detect a colony that is hidden below ground. Reproduced in color on Plate 5. Modified from Ken Gray Collection, courtesy of Oregon State University (#G182-0). Right: **Subterranean termite worker** (~0.25"). Notice how delicate this termite worker is. These worker termites are not adapted to exist outside the protected climate of the colony. Reproduced in color on Plate 5. Modified from Ken Gray Collection, courtesy of Oregon State University (#G163-30).

 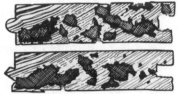

Left: **dampwood termite, winged reproductive** (~0.75–1.0"). This termite species is much larger and heavier than subterranean termites. Modified from Ken Gray Collection, courtesy of Oregon State University (#87-2). Right: **drywood termite damage**, cross section of wood flooring. Notice how the damage starts on the inside and moves toward the surface. This is typical of termite damage—the outside can be undamaged while the inside can be nearly hollow. Reproduced in color on Plate 5. Modified from H. B. Moore (1979), *Wood-Inhabiting Insects in Houses: Their Identification, Biology, Prevention and Control* (USDA, FS, DHUD publication).

important structural pests because of this requirement for damp, partially rotten wood. **Drywood termites,** on the other hand, have a much lower requirement for water; in fact, they can construct colonies in dry environments with no connection to a source of moisture at all. They do require higher temperatures than dampwood termites, so drywood termites occur in warm, dry climates such as the southwestern US. Drywood termites can be quite damaging because they often go undetected until the colonies are large. Finally, the **subterranean termites** construct

Termites actually digest wood fiber

Wood is made from fibers of a very tough material called **cellulose**. Cellulose fiber is what makes wood strong and flexible, and most paper is 100% cellulose. Almost no living organisms eat wood directly because it is so hard to digest cellulose. Try gnawing on a two-by-four, and you'll see what I mean. Most insects that tunnel in and damage wood are eating bits of other material, like starch, that are embedded in the wood fibers. Not termites. Termites actually eat the wood fiber itself and get all the nutrients they need to live. Termites can perform this little feat of cellulose digestion because of special microorganisms in their guts that attack cellulose and turn it into sugar. So, in exchange for a warm place to live, these microbes satisfy a termite's sweet tooth.

colonies underground on buried wood and extend the colony to our above-ground structures through tunnels, or shelter tubes, they construct. Subterranean termites, or "subs," are the termites that most people envisage if they think about termites.

All termites are small, delicate insects that live inside climate-controlled colonies that are constructed in the soil or in wood. Like other social insects, termite colonies are organized into castes with large reproductives and smaller workers and soldiers. Unlike other insects, termites actually eat wood, with the help of special microorganisms in their guts that convert wood fiber (cellulose) into sugar. Because termites consume the wood rather than just tunnel through it, over time a large termite colony can do extensive damage to wooden structures.

Subterranean termites live in underground colonies on buried wood. When the initial wood supply is depleted, the colony may be extended through **shelter tubes** to above-ground wood. This is when damage to structures occurs. Shelter tubes are made from soil particles and are therefore the color and texture of the local soil. The tubes are built on foundation walls, posts, pilings,

Termite baits

Termite baits are used to both monitor the activity of and eliminate certain kinds of termite colonies. The advantage of termite baits over soil treatments is that baiting uses far less insecticide and is less environmentally disruptive than conventional termite treatments. Some termite baits can be installed by homeowners but all systems are time-consuming to deploy and maintain.

Termite baiting works by tricking worker termites into taking poisoned bait back to the colony. Baits consist of some type of cellulose, the part of wood that termites need, that may be laced with insecticide or insect growth regulator. Foraging worker termites find the bait and recruit fellow nestmates to the new food source. The colony, and queen, are slowly poisoned when the toxin is taken back to the nest.

etc.—anything that spans the gap between soil and wood. Look for termite shelter tubes during annual inspections for insect and water damage; if tubes are found, it is an indication that subterranean termites may be active. Other major types of termites, such as drywood termites and dampwood termites, do not make shelter tubes.

Until recently, and since the end of World War II, subterranean termites were controlled in new and existing homes by treating the soil around the foundation with highly toxic and persistent insecticides like chlordane and heptachlor. These organochlorine insecticides were used in the US until they were banned in the 1980s. Nowadays, termite control uses lower toxicity organophosphate and pyrethroid insecticides; these are either applied to the soil to prevent new colony formation, or used in the form of termite baits that disrupt existing colonies.

Internet resources:

www.livingwithbugs.com/termite.html
www.livingwithbugs.com/termit_3.html (baits)

Chapter 3
Insects that swarm and sting

While most insects live solitary lives, a few have developed highly organized communities, or societies, where the work of the colony is performed by specialized castes. These are the **social insects**. Social insects live in colonies or hives where the various tasks of the colony—such as food gathering, colony defense, and reproduction—are carried out by specific members of the society, called *workers*, *soldiers*, *reproductives*, etc. The most familiar of the social insects are **ants, social wasps, bees**, and **termites**.

Some colonies of social insects become quite large, containing thousands of individuals. In order to defend the colony from predators such as skunks, bears, and others, a behavior called **swarming** has evolved to enable the colony to drive off these potential dangers. Swarming is similar to flocking behavior in birds,

Insect societies

In 1974, E. O. Wilson, professor of biology at Harvard University, published *Insect Societies,* a groundbreaking book describing the natural history of the **social insects**—ants, wasps, bees, and termites. In *Sociobiology: The New Synthesis* (1975), Professor Wilson uses social behavior in ants and other insects to help explain more complex social behavior in other animals including (somewhat controversially) humans. While he did not coin the term, Dr. Wilson's work popularized a whole new branch of science called **sociobiology.**

where large numbers of individuals attack a perceived threat to the group. If this swarming behavior is directed at us, these insects can become very dangerous. The term swarm can also refer to a non-defensive behavior in which some insects such as honey bees and termites start new colonies.

Ants, bees, and wasps all have a built-in defensive weapon protruding from their abdomen that is called a **stinger**. In some insects, the stinger is called an **ovipositor** and is used in placing eggs, (see horntail wasp, chapter 2, for a good example). The stinger in other insects is a hollow, sharply pointed needle that is attached to a venom gland. The stinger in bees is barbed and is pulled out of the bee during the act of stinging, which kills the bee. Wasp and ant stingers are not barbed and can be used over and over again. When insects sting they also inject a small volume of protein-rich venom into the wound.

Africanized honey bees (aka "killer bees")

The role of bees in natural ecosystems: Bees feed on plant nectar and pollen. In the act of collecting nectar and pollen, bees cross-pollinate plants.

There are a number of different strains, or subspecies, of the honey bee (*Apis millifera spp.*) that differ in terms of behavior and temperament. The European strain of honey bees is the one most people are familiar with and is called the **European honey bee**. This strain is fairly docile and usually does not aggressively defend its colony against invaders. This lack of aggressive defense is the reason that beekeepers can approach these colonies with minimal protection. However, the European honey bee is a relatively poor pollinator and honey producer, and is subject to a number of diseases and ectoparasites such as varroa mite.

In the 1950s a strain of honey bee was collected in Africa and taken to a lab in Brazil for study. This strain was a better honey producer and pollinator and was less affected by ectoparasites

A **bee beard** formed of European honey bees attracted to the queen bee, which is hidden beneath the mass of bees. This demonstration is commonly used to teach students how non-aggressive this strain of honey bee is, if handled correctly. Photo by J. D. DeAngelis.

than the European honey bee. Along with these desirable traits, this bee also exhibited a highly aggressive nature and would swarm and sting any threat to the colony. It was named the African strain or **African honey bee**. Researchers believed they could breed the aggressiveness out of the African strain by crossing it with the more docile European strain. Instead of a docile African strain, however, they ended up producing a highly aggressive European strain called the **Africanized honey bee**.

What happened next was the real disaster. The Africanized bees were accidentally released from the research apiary into the surrounding wild, and the colonies multiplied rapidly in the tropical climate of central Brazil. Since then, Africanized bees have slowly displaced native (European) honey bees wherever they occur together. Africanized bee colonies have moved steadily north, eventually reaching the southwestern US in the 1990s. At this point (2008), they occur throughout the southwestern US from southern California, Nevada, Arizona, southern New Mexico, southwest Texas and as far east as southern Florida. New Africanized colonies are found further north each year.

Stings from Africanized bees are individually no more dangerous than those from European bees, since the two bees are nearly identical. The difference is in the number of stings one is likely to receive during any encounter.

Nobody is certain how far north "killer bees" will eventually move. The two strains easily interbreed so colonies can be "Africanized" over time as more and more of the aggressive traits are bred into the European strain. Many researchers believe that the southern US will become entirely Africanized while the northern states will remain mostly populated by the native, European strain. There will likely be a transition zone between the two areas where individual hives will be more or less Africanized.

Homeowners should never attempt to control any honey bee hive. If you live in an area where Africanized colonies have been confirmed you should consult with local experts about removal of threatening hives. If you live in other areas, you can contact a local beekeeper—they will likely be happy to remove the beehive safely and add it to their stock.

Internet resources:

www.en.wikipedia.org/wiki/Africanized_honey_bee-
www.livingwithbugs.com/killer_bee.html

Fire ants and harvester ants (Formicidae)

The role of ants in natural ecosystems: Ants are predators and scavengers.

Worldwide there are many ant species that are dangerous. In some places a careless encounter with an agitated ant colony can even be fatal. A few particularly dangerous ants are the jack jumper, or bulldog, ants of Australia and the driver ants of Africa, a type of army ant. In the US, however, two ant species require particular caution—the **fire ants** and **harvester ants**.

Fire ants (*Solenopsis spp.*) are so named because of their painful sting, not their bite. Like their wasp cousins, ants have stingers. Some ants use their stingers in defense of the nest and to subdue prey. A few species, like fire ants, possess a highly potent sting that is able to drive off any animal intruder. In the US, fire ants and harvester ants (*Pogonomyrmex spp.*) are notorious for their painful stings. In order to drive their stingers deep into the wound both ants bite first to anchor themselves before plunging

Left: **fire ant mounds** in a pasture. Individual mounds can reach 18" in height. Photo by USDA/ APHIS/PPQ Archives. Right: **harvester ant mound**, eastern Oregon. These large, flat mounds are common in deserts, where rainfall is low and soils are gravelly. Harvester ants are red ants that forage on seeds, and vegetation is often cleared from around mounds, as in this photo. Standing or sitting on a mound of this type would be very dangerous! Reproduced in color on Plate 6. Modified from Ken Gray Collection, courtesy of Oregon State University (#363-31).

their stingers home. A small injection of venom, which causes the burning sensation and allergic reaction, completes the sting.

In the US the red imported fire ant, *Solenopsis invicta*, is a highly invasive species currently distributed across the South from coastal North Carolina to east Texas. Local infestations have been found west to California. Scientists have estimated that if the distribution of this ant continues to expand it could encompass all of central California and western Oregon.

The red imported fire ant is a small brown ant that can be difficult to distinguish from other small brown ants, unless you get stung. They make extremely large mound nests in fields, pastures, lawns, and along roads—these nests may reach 18" in height and contain thousands of ants. Fire ants are very effective predators. In fact, even though this ant is considered an invasive pest, when local fire ant populations are eliminated farmers have noticed a significant increase in other crop pests.

Fire ants are dangerous insects and should not be allowed to remain around homes or play areas. They have an extremely potent sting and a tendency to swarm at the least disturbance. The presence of mounds is the best indication that fire ants are in the area. *Do not attempt to collect ants for identification.*

Control of fire ants is usually a two step process—**baiting** and **individual mound treatment**. Fire ant baits look and smell like corn meal and have an oily texture. Conventional insecticides, even those marketed as baits, will be gray or brown in color with either no odor, or a chemical odor. True baits should be your first choice for long-term fire ant control. Baits can be broadcast with either a hand-operated spreader, or a push-type fertilizer spreader for very large areas. Treat infested areas in fall and/or spring when worker ants are active and there is no rain anticipated for at least 8 hours. Test for worker ant activity by carefully placing a small piece of hot dog next to a mound. If ants are active they will begin feeding within 30 minutes. Individual mounds that pose a particular hazard—such as any that are located in lawns, gardens, playgrounds, schools, parks, etc.—can be treated with insecticide, but for long-term area treatment true baits are best.

Harvester ants occur in dry deserts where the soils are relatively loose and gravelly. Individual harvester ant nests can be huge but most of the volume is underground. I once saw a resin cast of a harvester ant colony that had been made by pouring liquid resin into the mound, where it then hardened and the cast

Think of ants as *wasps without wings*

If you look carefully at an ant (see carpenter ants in chapter 2), you'll notice that it looks a lot like a wasp without wings (see social wasps in chapter 3). In fact, ants and wasps are very closely related. The shape of the body and head are very similar between the two, and most have a thin "waist" between the thorax and abdomen. Both insects have stingers that can be used in defense. And finally, all ants and many wasps live in highly organized colonies.

One "ant" is in fact technically a wingless wasp. You may have heard of velvet ants or "cow killer" ants. These large, fuzzy, brightly colored "ants" are actually wingless wasps (family Mutillidae) with a highly potent sting but they resemble large ants. (see www.en.wikipedia.org/wiki/Velvet_ant)

could be dug out. (Graduate students were "employed" to dig up the cast under the hot desert sun.) The main chamber was 5 feet deep with many large side chambers extending out 3 feet or more, and the researcher suspected that many of the smaller side chambers were missing.

The flat mound around the opening of harvester ant colonies is composed of loose rock brought up from below. Harvester ants forage on seeds and will not enter homes or cause any damage, so no control is necessary. They only pose a threat if you accidentally happen to stand on a mound, causing the ants to swarm and sting because they see you as an enemy. The researcher who made the cast of the colony described the sting of a harvester ant as a *memorable experience.*

Internet resources:

www.livingwithbugs.com/fire_ant.html
www.fireant.tamu.edu/ (Texas Imported Fire Ant Research and Management Project)

Social wasps (yellowjackets, paper wasps, hornets)

The role of social wasps in natural ecosystems: Like ants, social wasps are predators and scavengers. The species that are mostly scavengers are the ones that become pests.

Close-up of **wasp larvae** in cells. Some cells are uncapped, showing larvae inside; some cells are empty, waiting for an egg from the queen. Modified from Ken Gray Collection, courtesy of Oregon State University (#G159-11)

Wasps (Hymenoptera) are considered by scientists to be among the most evolutionarily advanced of the insects. They range in size from tiny **parasitic wasps** that develop *inside the bodies of aphids* to large **predatory hunters** capable of capturing and killing an animal as large as a tarantula spider. While most wasps are solitary insects and have contact with other members of their species only during mating season, some species are highly social insects that form complex colonies like other social insects such as bees, ants, and termites. Wasps that form these complex societies are called the **social wasps.** In the US, the social wasps are called **yellowjackets** (or sometimes **hornets**) and **paper wasps,** while in the rest of the world they are called social wasps, social vespids (Vespidae is the social wasp family) or just wasps. Like other Hymenoptera (ants, bees, and wasps) wasps possess a potent stinger, and because social wasps aggressively defend their large colonies, they can sometimes pose a threat to people.

Yellowjacket wasps (*Vespula* and *Dolichovespula spp.***)** have a distinctive black-and-yellow or black-and-white coloration. These wasps vary in size from about ½" long to perhaps ¾" long and they lack the *dense* covering of fine hairs that clothe bees. When viewed from the side, they look more like ants—and ants and wasps are closely related, in fact. The most noticeable

Stingers deliver eggs and/or venom

The wasp stinger is a sharp, hollow, needle-like structure at the tip of the abdomen, that can be used to carefully place eggs or deliver a painful and sometimes deadly stab to an enemy or prey. When the stinger is used to place eggs, it is called an **ovipositor** and egg-laying is called **oviposition.** The stinger is also attached to a **venom gland,** so along with a painful stab the stinger can be used to inject a drop of venom. The venom is used mainly to subdue prey, but a small percentage of people are so highly allergic to wasp venom that even a few stings can create a life-threatening condition called anaphylactic shock.

Above: **yellowjacket (Vespidae) wasp** (~0.5"). The biggest difference between paper wasps and yellowjacket wasps can be seen in this photograph. *The hind legs of yellowjacket wasps are short* compared to those of paper wasps, which tend to hang down in flight. Modified from Ken Gray Collection, courtesy of Oregon State University (#383-16). Right: Large, papery **yellowjacket, or social wasp, nest.** Notice how the cells are not visible—they are completely enclosed in the papery envelope. Compare the yellowjacket wasp nest to photos of paper wasp nests, which have an open architecture, with the cells exposed. The nest in this photo grew to roughly the size of a soccer ball by the end of the season. Photo by J. D. DeAngelis. Reproduced in color on Plate 7.

characteristic of yellowjacket wasps, however, is the size and type of nests they construct.

Like other social insects, yellowjacket wasps build large nests that can hold *thousands* of individuals. The nests are constructed of a papery material that the wasps make from wood. They peel the wood from trees and unpainted outdoor wooden articles around the house, such as decks and furniture. This is why the nests often take on the colors of nearby wood. These nests can either be built above ground as shown in these pictures or be buried below ground, with only a single entrance hole leading to the nest. In either case, except for the entrance, the **nests are completely enclosed by a paper envelope**; when you look at a yellowjacket nest, you can't see individual cells as you can with those of other wasps (see, for example, the photo of a paper wasp nest later in this section).

Nest construction begins in the spring and nests "die" the following fall with the first hard frost. The only members of a colony to survive through the winter are the reproductive queen

Is it a hornet, a yellowjacket, or a bee?

In the US, it is technically wrong to use the term **hornet** when referring to most yellowjacket wasps, because there is only one true hornet species in this country. Even the **bald-faced hornet** is technically a yellowjacket—it belongs to the genus *Dolichovespula,* which includes other true yellowjacket wasps. True hornets belong to the genus *Vespa* which has only one species in North America, *Vespa crabro,* the European hornet. While this distinction is really only of much interest to entomologists, it explains why some people insist on using the name **yellowjacket** rather than hornet.

On the other hand, the distinction between **bees** and **wasps** is a more fundamental and important one, and it is therefore more annoying to an entomologist when the terms are misused. The term **bee** should *only* be used for insects such as honey bees or bumble bees. Bees can be distinguished from wasps because bees generally have a dense covering of fine hairs that are used for collecting pollen, whereas wasps are shiny with a much less dense coat. Bees collect pollen and plant nectar, whereas wasps are predators and scavengers on other animals. As far as their behavior, bees tend to be docile and only rarely sting, whereas social wasps are very territorial and aggressive, especially near their nests.

yellowjackets that will start new colonies in the spring. For most species, all other members of the colony die with the onset of winter. A few species like the German yellowjacket (*Vespula germanica*) make a perennial nest that can exist for many years and grow to an enormous size, often in association with a heated building. All nests grow throughout the spring and summer and generally reach their peak size in late summer and early fall.

Like other wasps, the social wasps are mostly **beneficial insects**. They prey on other insects, including many pest species, and they scavenge the carcasses of dead animals, thus acting as a kind of natural sanitation service. Sometimes, however, they can be a pest if their activity, or ours, brings them into contact with us. Any

Colorful yellowjacket nest. Notice how the paper nest is similar in color to the surrounding wood that was used to make the nest paper. Photo by J. D. DeAngelis. Reproduced in color on Plate 7.

large wasp nest can be dangerous if accidentally bumped or stepped on. Nests that are built near sites of human activity—such as in a garden or playground—pose a threat, especially in late summer when nests are at maximum size. Those species that have adopted a mainly scavenger lifestyle can be especially threatening, because these species make large nests and foraging wasps are attracted to any outdoor activity that includes open food containers.

Scavengers versus predators

In the animal world, **predators** eat live prey while **scavengers** feed on dead animal or vegetable matter. Few animals, however, are strict scavengers or predators. Lions and tigers, for example, are mostly predatory but will consume an already dead animal if the carcass is fairly fresh. Likewise, eagles prefer live prey but also scavenge carrion. In the insect world, the line between scavenger and predator is often a bit more clearly defined. Predatory insects such as certain yellowjacket wasps rarely if ever feed on dead animals, and scavenger species generally scavenge for food rather then attack living prey. There are four species of mainly scavenger yellowjacket wasps that cause most of the problems worldwide. These are the wasps that come around whenever food is exposed outdoors, especially in late summer. These scavenger species are listed in Table 2.

Table 2: Where are the scavenger yellowjackets?

Region	Common yellowjacket (Vespula vulgaris)	German yellowjacket (Vespula germanica)	Western yellowjacket (Vespula pensylvanica)	Eastern yellowjacket (Vespula maculifons)
worldwide	■	■		
western US, western Canada, Hawaii	■	■	■	■
south & eastern US, central (midwest) US	■	■		■

When it becomes necessary to destroy a threatening wasp nest, you should proceed carefully. Both types of nests (in-ground and above ground) can be treated with an **aerosol insecticide** made for this type of application. Look for an aerosol insecticide called something like "Wasp and Hornet Spray." *Never use other types of liquids to treat nests.* Treat the nest in the evening when wasp activity is at a minimum but before it gets too dark. You don't want to be stumbling around in the dark near an angry wasp nest.

The familiar wasp traps that attract foraging wasps with sweets, meat, or artificial attractants are only marginally useful for reducing wasp numbers. The problem is that the traps simply can't attract and capture enough workers (compared to the number produced by a large nest) to make much of a difference. The best use of traps is as decoys to temporarily move wasp activity away from an outdoor event (see Internet resources).

Paper wasps (*Polistes spp.*) also form colonies with a division of labor, but these colonies are generally smaller and less organized than those of yellowjacket wasps. Paper wasps also are less

Left: **European paper wasp nests**, built under the flap of a trashcan liner. Notice how individual cells are visible, not enclosed in a paper envelope as they are in yellowjacket nests. Photo by E. A. DeAngelis. Right: **European paper wasp** (*Polistes dominulus*). Notice how similar this paper wasp is to the yellowjacket. Photo by J. D. DeAngelis. Reproduced in color on Plate 6.

aggressive, possibly because the colonies are smaller. Paper wasps are predators, so will not be pests at picnics and other outdoor activities where food is exposed. They make a smaller, open nest that is often seen suspended from the eaves of homes. Even though they can sting like other wasps, *paper wasps are generally harmless and can be left alone.*

There is a relatively new paper wasp species in the US that came here accidentally from continental Europe, probably in the early 1980s. Called the **European paper wasp** (*Polistes dominulus*), it is a little different from our native species and sometimes behaves a bit like a yellowjacket wasp. The European paper wasp nests are larger than our native paper wasps, wasp activity starts earlier in the spring, and the wasps themselves can be more aggressive than typical paper wasps. Worst of all, this new paper wasp can become a real nuisance because it builds nests in every nook and cranny around homes—and is in some areas it seems to be displacing the native species. Because the European paper wasp arrived without any of its natural enemies, its populations have increased unchecked. But fear not—sooner or later some disease or parasite will likely discover this new resource and bring this invader under natural control.

Internet resources:

www.livingwithbugs.com/yellow.html (yellowjacket wasps)
www.livingwithbugs.com/yel_trap.html (using traps)
www.livingwithbugs.com/epw.html (European paper wasp)

Chapter 4
Insects that invade kitchens and pantries

Certain insects invade kitchens and pantries *because that's where the food is stored*. Some specialize in infesting the food we store in kitchens, pantries, and warehouses. Scientists call these the **stored-product pests**. While some insects infest the stored food-stuff itself, some only enter kitchens in search of spilled food or discarded scraps and generally won't infest food that is properly stored. Ants and cockroaches are examples of insects that will take advantage of situations that we create for them through improper food handling, while flour and grain beetles and meal moths are true stored-product pests and can infest even properly stored food.

Nuisance ants (Formicidae)

The role of ants in natural ecosystems: Ants are predators and scavengers.

The most important thing to know about ants in general is that they live in **highly organized societies** (see chapter 3). The various functions of the society—food gathering, colony defense, colony construction, the tending of young, and reproduction—are carried out by individual ants that are assigned these tasks by a "monarch," usually called the **queen ant**. Queen ants are females and the only members of the society that lay eggs. The other principal caste is the **worker ants**. The worker caste are all

Left: trailing behavior in **nuisance ants**. Notice that ants are following an invisible "trail" to the food source. Drawing by E. A. DeAngelis. Right: household **nuisance ants** (probably odorous house ants) feeding at a homemade bait station. Photo by J. D. DeAngelis.

females, too, but they never mate or lay eggs. The sole function of workers is to serve the colony. The last caste is made up of the male ants or **drones**. Drones have short lives and only appear in the colony long enough to mate with newly matured queens. New queens and drones have wings that enable them to fly away from their birth colony prior to mating in an event called the nuptial flight.

Scientists call insects that form complex, task-organized colonies the social insects (most insects, on the other hand, are non-social). Ants, some bees, some wasps, and termites are the highly social, or **eusocial**, insects. Ants, bees, and wasps all belong to the same insect order, **Hymenoptera**, whereas termites belong to another order, the **Isoptera**. The cooperation between colony mates allows social insects to exploit new habitats. *It can also make them a formidable pest.*

Ants build colonies in a wide variety of substrates. Many species nest in the soil, while some nest above ground. Ants that nest above ground can be particularly troublesome, since they sometimes build their nests in our homes. Soil-nesting species can also use our homes as foraging grounds, where they come to look for food and water.

The diet of ants is extremely diverse as well. Many species prefer sweet, high-carbohydrate liquids such as honeydew and plant nectar, while at other times they need a more meat-based, protein-rich diet. Dietary preference is largely determined by the needs of developing larvae in the colony.

Individual colonies can survive for many years. If the queen dies, she can be replaced from the developing larvae. Colonies continue to grow and expand if left unchecked. Some species even undergo a process called budding in which a large colony splits in two. These split-off colonies may or may not have their own queen. If the budded colony is without a queen of its own, it may remain as a satellite colony, in continuous contact with the parent colony.

My wife Elizabeth has a cousin who is an avid birdwatcher. She tells us that birdwatchers refer to all nondescript, small birds as Little Brown Birds, or LBBs for short. There are, apparently, quite a few species of little birds that look so alike that even experienced birdwatchers can't easily tell them apart. This same logic can be applied to several species of small, brown ants that invade homes, do no particular damage, but cause great concern because

Avoiding problems with home-invading ants

Ants have a *sweet tooth*. While fats, oils, and proteins are sought at some times of the year, **sugar** is universally accepted by ants. As any homeowner knows, ants will find even small amounts of spilled sugar or syrup. Once a bit of sugary food is found by a foraging ant, it races back to the colony and recruits nestmates to the food source, much like a honey bee that has found a good source of flower nectar. We can use this behavior against them by enticing workers into taking back to the nest sweet **baits** that have been laced with insecticide. Boric acid or various **insect growth regulators** are used as the insecticide in these baits.

Do not use insecticidal aerosol sprays for home-invading ants. These sprays only disperse colonies and may actually make matters worse. Explore the Internet resources at the end of the chapter for updated information about ant control using professional and homemade baits.

Insect growth regulators (IGRs)

Insect growth regulators (IGRs) are compounds that interfere with an insect's ability to grow or reproduce. For example, the chemical **methoprene** is widely used in pest control to stop certain immature insects from completing their development into adults. IGRs tend to be relatively non-toxic to other animals and can be effectively used at very low dosage, which makes them environmentally friendly.

of their sheer numbers. They all look pretty much the same, have somewhat similar behavior, and the approach to their management is similar. We can call them **little brown nuisance ants**, or LBNAs for short. Worldwide, the most common home-invading ants are the pharaoh ant (*Monomorium pharaonis*), the Argentine ant (*Linepithema humile*), the odorous house ant (*Tapinoma sessile*), the pavement ant (*Tetramorium caespitum*), and a few others.

Pharaoh ants occur worldwide in association with houses, warehouses, and other buildings. This ant does not nest outdoors except in southern latitudes and has been able to adapt to field conditions in southern Florida. In colder climates, it has become established in heated buildings.

Argentine ants are native to central South America but are now found in many Mediterranean and subtropical climates throughout the world; this ant is considered a highly invasive pest in many countries of the southern hemisphere and warmer parts of the northern hemisphere. In the US, highly invasive pest populations are found in the southeastern and West Coast states, especially California, and in parts of Hawaii.

Odorous house ants occur throughout the US. They give off a strong coconut-like odor when crushed. This species is commonly found indoors in large numbers. They nest in soil and inside structures.

Pavement ants are common in the eastern US but can also be found throughout the country. This species probably originated in Europe.

Ant baits

Ant baits are made of a food base, usually some type of carbohydrate (sugar) mixed with an insecticide. Boric acid (see later this chapter) in the form of borate is commonly used, but insect growth regulators are used as well. Baits should be placed along the avenues, or trails, that ants use. Trails are established by foraging ants when a food source is found. As the forager travels back to the colony, it lays down a chemical marker that other ants can follow to the food source. When placing bait stations, try not to disturb these trails and never wash them away, or spray them with insecticide, as this will discourage ants from visiting the bait. See the Internet resources at the end of this chapter for sources of commercial and homemade baits.

Outdoor **perimeter foundation sprays** can also be used to prevent soil-nesting ants from foraging inside a structure. Insecticide should be sprayed onto the part of the exterior foundation between the soil and the bottom of the exterior siding. These applications are only needed when ants are moving between an outdoor nest and the interior. Because many indoor infestations originate from colonies located in interior walls, outside foundation sprays will have no effect on the movement of these ants.

Internet resources:

www.livingwithbugs.com/nui_ants.html
www.ipm.ucdavis.edu/PMG/PESTNOTES/pn7411.html
www.ohioline.osu.edu/hyg-fact/2000/2064.html

Others: Google the common nuisance ant species such as pharaoh ant, Argentine ant, odorous house ant, or pavement ant.

Beetles (Coleoptera)

Lots of different beetles infest whole grains, flour, or products made from grains and flour. Beetles also infest other food products like dried fruit, nuts, pet food, and so forth. Damage from these pests can be extensive, but fortunately it is usually pretty easy to avoid damage and does not involve poisonous pesticides or traps. These beetles, and stored-product pests in general, can gain a foothold when food is stored too long before it is used. In warehouses these pests are rarely a problem, as long as stock is properly rotated so that individual units are not stored too long. For homeowners, the rule is: *don't store packaged foods, even unopened packages, for longer than about 2 months*, unless the unopened package is frozen for several days first.

As their name might suggest, **carpet beetles** are most often thought of (if you think of them at all) as potential pests of carpets made from wool and similar natural fibers. However, certain carpet beetles are actually more often found in kitchens and

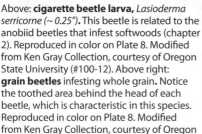

Above: **cigarette beetle larva,** *Lasioderma serricorne (~ 0.25")*. This beetle is related to the anobiid beetles that infest softwoods (chapter 2). Reproduced in color on Plate 8. Modified from Ken Gray Collection, courtesy of Oregon State University (#100-12). Above right: **grain beetles** infesting whole grain. Notice the toothed area behind the head of each beetle, which is characteristic of this species. Reproduced in color on Plate 8. Modified from Ken Gray Collection, courtesy of Oregon State University (#36-16). Right: close-up of **carpet beetle (Dermestidae) larva (~0.16").** Notice how fuzzy this larva appears in comparison with the larva of the cigarette beetle, which belongs to a different family. Reproduced in color on Plate 8. Modified from Ken Gray Collection, courtesy of Oregon State University (#113-10).

pantries, where they infest a wide variety of stored foods such as cereal, grains, nuts, dry pet food, and spices.

Carpet beetles are small (⅛"), rounded beetles that are sometimes black but may also have brown or white scales. Adult beetles are found outdoors, where they feed on plant pollen. The larvae are small, fuzzy grubs that infest stored food products and can damage certain fabrics. You may first notice carpet beetles when you uncover the fuzzy larval skins in drawers and cupboards. As larvae grow, they periodically shed their old skins and these can remain in place for months or years until cleaned away.

Cleaning is the best way to control carpet beetle larvae, whether they are infesting fabrics or stored food. Insecticides are usually not necessary. Carefully examine storage areas and discard any infested food. Discard food even if you only slightly suspect that it is infested. Next, clean shelves with a mild household cleaner. Unlike meal moths, another pantry-type pest, there

Freezing kills all stages of pantry pests

Even unopened packages of some foods from the grocery store can contain a small number of live insects or eggs. These products are perfectly safe to use, but if they are stored for too long, the insects can multiply and eventually ruin the food, or start a pantry infestation. A simple visit to the freezer is usually enough to eliminate all stages (eggs, larvae, adults) of pantry pests such as meal moths, flour and grain beetles, and the cigarette and drugstore beetles. As long as the package is tightly sealed, it can be removed from the freezer after about 2 days and will remain bug-free for a long time. This treatment will not protect against normal spoilage but it will prevent most insect pests from ruining your stored food products. In our home, we routinely put new bags of pet food, bird seed, nuts, dried fruit (raisins, etc.) through this procedure before moving the packages to the pantry. Access to a large chest or walk-in freezer really helps. Many museums now use the same procedure to protect displays, such as animal hides and pinned insects, from these same pests.

Why is flour sifted?

As recently as the 1930s, flour-mill operators believed that **flour beetles** developed spontaneously from the flour. In some parts of a typical mill, beetle larvae were so abundant that they *turned the flour gray*. Even today, the US Food and Drug Administration allows up to about 40 insect fragments per ounce of milled flour as a safe limit in the US food supply. This takes into account the fact that when you grind any whole grain, such as wheat, there is a possibility that small amounts of foreign substances that might have contaminated the grain, including insects, will be present. So long as the amount is kept small, these contaminants are completely harmless.

Sifting of milled grains (flour) has two purposes—to reverse the packing that occurs during storage, so that a consistent volume can be measured, and to remove contaminants such as insects and inorganic grit. Nowadays, the quantity of insects and other contaminants in flour is pretty small, so sifting is not as important, but in the past it might have kept your breakfast roll from walking off the plate.

are no traps available for the carpet beetles that infest kitchens.

Grain beetles are small, brownish-colored insects about $\frac{1}{10}$" long. Grain beetles can be common anywhere food is stored, including commercial warehouses and grain storage silos. They infest cereals, meal, grains, dried fruits, flour, macaroni, spices, herbs, dried meats, nuts, crackers, dry pet food, and other foodstuffs. As with carpet beetles, the simplest and most effective control measure is to locate the source of infestation and quickly dispose of it.

Internet resources:

www.livingwithbugs.com/carpet_beetle.html
www.livingwithbugs.com/pantry_pest.html
www.ohioline.osu.edu/hyg-fact/2000/2083.html
www.ohioline.osu.edu/hyg-fact/2000/2086.html

Cockroaches

The role of cockroaches in natural ecosystems: Cockroaches are world champion scavengers and recyclers. Cockroaches are able to survive on almost any scrap of plant or animal food; a few are even able to digest cellulose like termites.

Believe it or not, most species of cockroaches are not pests. They are natural components of the ecosystem, like other insects. They go about their business unnoticed. Cockroaches are mainly tropical insects; only a few species are native to North America. The cockroach species that we consider pests (American cockroach, German cockroach, brownbanded cockroach, and a few others) are tropical species that have adapted to exploiting the food and water resources we give them. These pest species are the ultimate scavengers. They will feed on almost any type of vegetable or animal matter, fresh or spoiled. They are just as happy dining on scraps and crumbs they find in your kitchen, as on the week-old garbage in the dumpster behind the restaurant. Give them a little food and water and their population will grow and grow.

Cockroaches are medium- to large-sized, light-brown to black insects. They are often associated with unsanitary urban environments but many species are not associated with human dwellings at all. Those species that do invade dwellings are called *peridomestic* (= near or in human dwellings) species. Peridomestic species enter buildings in search of **food and water.** Almost any foodstuff can attract and support cockroaches, because they are not very finicky in terms of what they like to eat. Populations can grow quickly in a building where adequate food and water are present. While cockroaches *do not cause structural damage,* their presence often indicates conditions that may be unhealthy. There are also concerns about cockroaches directly triggering allergic reactions, including asthma, and spreading disease by contaminating food.

Cockroaches and termites (chapter 2) are closely related—in fact, some scientists consider termites to be a type of wood-eating cockroach. However, cockroaches do not form complex colonies

Above: **American cockroach nymph**, aka palmetto
bug, *Periplaneta americana* (~1.0" excluding antennae).
This is the largest cockroach that infests homes in the
US. Reproduced in color on Plate 9. Modified from Ken
Gray Collection, courtesy of Oregon State University
(#G172-10). Above right: **German cockroach** (*Blattella
germanica*). This roach is relatively easy to recognize
because of the two dark strips behind the head. Reproduced in color on Plate 9. Modified
from Ken Gray Collection, courtesy of Oregon State University (#G172-20). Right: **cockroach
egg cases** (each about ~0.2"). These single cases contain many individual eggs. Some cockroach species can be identified based on egg cases alone. Reproduced in color on Plate 9.
Modified from Ken Gray Collection, courtesy of Oregon State University (#G173-33).

like termites, though they do live together in groups. They prefer
warm and damp areas in out-of-the-way places; these are called
harborages. Cockroach activity is usually highest at night, when
light levels are low. In fact, cockroach activity in the open, during the day, typically indicates very high populations, because it
indicates that individuals have been pushed out of harborages
because of overcrowding.

Effective cockroach control must include **elimination of food
and water sources**, as much as possible, and the use of **poison baits**,
traps, and/or **insecticides**. For infestations in commercial buildings,

Cockroach in other languages

Cockroaches are pests in human dwellings almost everywhere and
most languages have a word for them. For example, in Norwegian a
cockroach is called **kakerlakk**, in German **Küchenschabe**, **cucaracha**
in Spanish, **csótány** in Hungarian, **blatte** or **cafard** in French, **barata**
in Portuguese, **karaluch** in Polish, **scarafaggio** or **blatta** in Italian
(blatta is also the Latin name), and **zhangláng** in Chinese.

Peridomestic cockroaches in the desert

Cockroaches can be severe pests in the southwestern and south-eastern states where warm temperatures allow them to survive year round outdoors. In the desert southwest, dry summers would normally prevent cockroaches from surviving outdoors. However, the availability of water used in landscaping creates islands of wet tropical climate in the middle of an otherwise dry desert. If this warm and wet climate is combined with a food source (such as pet food, garbage, etc.), there is potential for an explosive growth in the cockroach population.

For example, the city of Las Vegas sits in one of the driest deserts on earth, yet there are pockets of severe cockroach infestation scattered around the city. Why? Is Las Vegas particularly unsanitary? Or does it have something to do with the sin in "sin city"? No. It is because the warm climate and water sources allow cockroaches to live outside and invade homes *from the outside*. This does not occur in colder climates, or in dry climates under normal conditions, because tropical cockroaches don't survive in large numbers under dry or cold conditions. The cockroaches in Las Vegas survive and multiply outside because of the **availability of water used in landscaping**. If water use outdoors was reduced, especially water used for lawns and landscape plants, cockroach populations would decline.

such as restaurants or apartment buildings, sanitation should be combined with baiting, as well as "crack and crevice" treatments.

Pest species of cockroaches are normally confined to heated buildings, because these insects are adapted to living in warm and wet tropical, or semi-tropical, climates. Peridomestic species don't survive outdoors where it freezes in winter or is too dry in summer. Our buildings and homes provide cockroaches with everything they need—warmth, water, food, and shelter from natural enemies.

The key to understanding peridomestic cockroaches is the availability of food and water. Because cockroaches are so well adapted to exploiting these resources, even limited amounts of food and water can support a thriving population. You must *eliminate sources of accessible food and water* to have any chance of controlling an infestation of peridomestic cockroaches, especially in warmer climates. Because treatments to control cockroaches in commercial buildings are generally more aggressive than in a single-family home, different approaches are used.

Cockroach control in single-family homes should be relatively simple because you, the homeowner, can control what happens in every room. If you eliminate sources of accessible food and water in every part of the house, you can achieve control with easy-to-use—and inexpensive—baits and dust insecticides. *Don't use aerosol sprays, as these will just cause roaches to scatter and make baits ineffective.*

First, **eliminate sources of food and water**. Be ruthless—clean any exposed sources of cooking grease, sugars, and other foodstuffs. Also repair leaky pipes and other sources of water. Cleaning and water source elimination is the most important part of cockroach control. Second, apply a borate powder insecticide ("roach

Borate insecticide

Borate, also called borax, is a mineral mined from the earth. Borate mining was made famous by the "twenty-mule team wagons" that hauled borax across the Mojave Desert in the 1880s from the mine in Death Valley, California. Borate is a salt of boric acid and has many commercial uses, from soap to glass making. It is also an effective **natural insecticide, fungicide**, and **wood preservative**. It turns out that borate is highly toxic to insects and fungi but is practically nontoxic to mammals, including us.

Borate insecticides are available as powders or liquids. Powders are generally used dry and simply sprinkled in the path of the pest, so that particles of borate are picked up as the insect walks through the powder. Borate is soluble in water, so it can also be used as the poison in baits—for example, ant baits—or applied to wood as a preservative (chapter 2).

Cockroach baits

Like baits that are used for ant control, cockroach baits are a mixture of some type of food plus an insecticide or insect growth regulator. Cockroach baits are often formulated as a gel that is applied with a applicator that looks like a large plastic syringe without the sharp needle. Baits are much more effective and safer to use than conventional insecticide sprays for cockroach control.

powder") in places where cockroaches travel. Cockroaches, and many other pests, follow walls, only rarely venturing out into the room. Place a *light dusting* of **borate powder** behind appliances and cabinets and under sinks, etc. Replace this powder when it is disturbed. Finally, cockroach baits can be used in these same areas, but don't use aerosol sprays. Most of the time you can skip the use of baits in single-family dwellings if you have done a good job of sanitation and water source control.

Cockroach infestations in commercial buildings are more difficult to eliminate because typically you cannot control what happens in every part of the building. If there are areas of the building that are not cleaned and treated, for whatever reason, these can serve as continual sources of cockroaches that reinfest the building. In commercial buildings, therefore, it may be necessary to treat areas that are accessible with residual insecticides and aggressively use commercial baits to disrupt the populations in other parts of the building. It is possible that you won't be able to achieve complete elimination of the cockroach population; you may have to be content with only suppression.

Internet resources:

www.livingwithbugs.com/cockroach_identification.html

Meal or pantry moths (Lepidoptera)

The role of meal moths in natural ecosystems: Most moths and butterflies (Lepidoptera) feed on plants in one form or another. Meal moths have adapted to feeding on dried fruits, grains, nuts, and seeds.

The dark-colored little moth that fluttered out of your kitchen cabinet probably startled you. When you saw the second one you started to figure you might have a problem. This small moth did not come indoors from outside; it developed inside your cabinet on dry stored-foods such as cereals, grains, dried fruit, and dry pet food (a moth favorite). The moth is called a **meal moth**; it is one of the most common pests of stored food worldwide. Meal moths are serious pests of stored-food products from kitchens and pantries to warehouses. Their larvae infest a wide variety of coarse-grained food products, such as dry pet food, nuts, seeds, dried fruit, and coarse grains like cornmeal. As larvae feed, they may spin a **silken webbing** over the surface of the infested product. If you open a bag of dry pet food that has not been opened in a while and the surface is covered with fine webbing—it's not spiders, it's meal moths.

Worldwide there are a number of related moths that infest stored food products from milled grains or flour to dried fruit, nuts, and even tobacco. Larvae can cause spoilage by introducing

Left: **Indian meal moth** (*Plodia interpunctella*). Note the dark, coppery band across the wings. Adult moths are about ⅝" across the wings. Reproduced in color on Plate 10. Modified from Ken Gray Collection, courtesy of Oregon State University (#142-7). Right: **Indian meal moth larva.** Notice the frass and webbing on raisin. Reproduced in color on Plate 10. Modified from Ken Gray Collection, courtesy of Oregon State University (# G3-18.

Pheromone traps

Pheromones are chemicals that insects use to attract a mate or send some other kind of signal to members of their own species. For example, some insects produce *alarm pheromones* to warn other colony members of danger. Some female moths use pheromones to attract males of their own species. Females release their "perfume," and males follow the scent to where the female is waiting. We can use artificial pheromones to fool male moths into entering a trap, often just a sticky surface, from which they cannot escape. Pheromone traps can be used to detect an infestation at an early stage; they can also sometimes be used to reduce the population and achieve some level of control.

moisture and their own wastes; they can chew through thin plastic, so food stored in lightweight produce bags is not safe. For long-term storage use heavy plastic containers or glass.

If you see moths fluttering around the kitchen, you'll first need to locate the infestation. One of the best ways to locate infestations of meal moths is to use *pheromone traps to trap male moths*. Sticky pheromone traps employ a scent that mimics the female moth and attracts males. If male moths are trapped you can assume an infestation is nearby. Begin looking through your packaged foods—and be thorough. Don't overlook places where food might accumulate if spilled. Spilled pet food is a prime site of overlooked infestations. One mysterious infestation I was consulted about turned out to be caused by a teenager hiding food in his room. It took months for his parents to track down the source. Once found, infestations can be eliminated by discarding infested food and/or freezing anything that is suspect (see section on Beetles earlier in this chapter). Do not use insecticides in the kitchen or pantry; they won't be effective and can be hazardous when used indoors.

Internet resources:

www.livingwithbugs.com/mealmoth.html

Chapter 5
Insects that damage natural fabrics

Nowadays most textiles are made from synthetics such as nylon or polyester. Besides being relatively inexpensive to produce, synthetic fabrics are far more versatile, comfortable, and immune from insect attack. Natural-fiber textiles are made either from **plant fibers**, such as cotton or linen, or from **animal fibers** such as wool and silk. Plant fibers are composed of cellulose, a type of tough, long-chain carbohydrate, while animal fibers and hide are mostly protein. The distinction between plant-based textiles, such as cotton and linen, and animal-based textiles and leather is an important one, because some insects that damage textiles only feed on animal-based textiles (wool, silk, leather) and leave plant-based fabrics alone. Others will feed on and damage both plant-based and animal-based fabrics. Two insects that are notorious for damaging natural textiles are **carpet beetles** and **clothes moths**. Carpet beetles also infest stored food (chapter 4), and are more commonly pests in kitchens than in clothes closets.

As synthetic fabrics became more common after World War II, the insects that feed on wool, silk, and leather have diminished in everyday significance. We no longer routinely mothproof our winter clothing because a lot of it is made from synthetics. Likewise, few people have wool carpets in their homes anymore. However, as the percentage of natural-fiber textiles in our closets has shrunk, the value of individual pieces has increased— expensive, imported wool rugs and wall hangings, for example, are more common today.

Carpet beetles (Dermestidae)

The role of dermestid beetles in natural ecosystems: These beetles feed on the remains of dead animals.

Warning: this next part is a little gross, but you will see the point shortly. Within minutes after an animal dies outdoors, certain flies are attracted to the body and lay eggs on it. Fly maggots develop on the rotting flesh for several days to a week or so and consume the soft parts of the body. What's left after this process is mostly bone, hide and fur. The next group of insects to move in and exploit these remains are beetles that clean bones and consume hair and hide. These beetles belong to the family Dermestidae, or the dermestids. Certain dermestid beetles have adapted from eating the remains of animal carcasses to feeding on fabrics and products that are made from dead animals, such as fur, hide, silk (a product of moth larvae), wool, animal horn, etc. **Carpet beetles** are dermestids that have made this switch from dead animal recyclers to household pests.

There are four common carpet beetles that infest households. All are less than ¼" long; some are a uniformly dark color, while others have colored scales on their backs. Carpet beetles have a

Dermestid beetles and bone collectors

If you've ever seen a display of a real "live" skeleton (not a fossil), you've seen the handiwork of dermestid beetles. People who prepare bones for display (such as those used in a Biology 101 class) use dermestid beetle larvae to clean the flesh from the bones. The process is stinky but very effective. Bones and flesh from a dismembered carcass are placed in a chamber with dermestid beetle larvae. The larvae feed on everything *except* bone and after a time the bones are removed and have been cleaned of all flesh down to the smallest crack and crevice. The cleaned skeletal bones are then bleached and reassembled with wire. This method of cleaning bones is used by museums and other "bone collectors" worldwide.

Left: **black carpet beetle,** *Attagenus unicolor,* (~0.20"). Reproduced in color on Plate 10. Modified from Ken Gray Collection, courtesy of Oregon State University (#466-0). Right: **carpet beetle larva**. Notice the long fuzzy "tails." Reproduced in color on Plate 10. Modified from Ken Gray Collection, courtesy of Oregon State University (#267-11)

very distinctive larval stage; this is the stage that people most often encounter, either as live larvae or in the form of cast-off skins (since larvae, like all insects, shed their skins as they grow). Carpet beetle larvae are fuzzy-looking with long bristly hairs. Adult beetles feed on plant pollen and nectar and so are found outdoors, while the larvae feed on a variety of animal and plant materials.

Fuzzy carpet beetle larvae feed on, and damage, wool, fur, hide, animal horn, feathers, hair, silk, linen, cotton, and rayon. Soiled fabrics are much more likely to attract carpet beetle feeding. Carpet beetle larvae also infest stored food items such as cereal, grains, nuts, dry pet food, and spices (see chapter 4).

Cleaning is the best way to control carpet beetle larvae that are damaging wool carpets or rugs. Insecticides are usually not necessary. Thoroughly clean wool carpets and rugs. Be sure to move furniture and clean the area under the legs of the furniture, because carpet beetles prefer these hidden areas. If you find fuzzy carpet beetle larvae or shed skins in kitchen cabinets, this indicates a food storage, or pantry, infestation. Carefully examine storage areas and discard infested food. Clean shelves with a mild household cleaner. Don't use insecticides in the kitchen.

Normal dry cleaning, or freezing for several days, will kill all stages of carpet beetles in clothing. Clothes that are regularly worn and laundered will not support a carpet beetle infestation. For long-term storage, clean clothes can be placed in airtight plastic storage boxes. There's no need to use mothballs (see chapter 12) in storage or closets; recent studies have warned about the toxic effects of mothball use. Control of a carpet beetle infestation in a clothes closet can be a long-term project, so you'll need patience. Carefully inspect and clean areas of suspected infestation. Stick with it and you'll eventually eliminate these pesky pests.

Internet resources:

www.livingwithbugs.com/carpet_beetle.html
www.ohioline.osu.edu/hyg-fact/2000/2083.html

Clothes moths (Tineidae)

The role of tineid moths in natural ecosystems: While most moths feed on plants in one form or another, clothes moths have adapted to feeding on dried animal protein such as wool.

Clothes moth larvae, like carpet beetle larvae, feed on a variety of dried animal protein such as skin, hair, and horn. And like dermestid beetles, clothes moths are adapted to exploiting the remains of dead animals. The jump from animal remains to fabrics made from animal protein is not a big one; it probably occurred when ancient people began to use animal skins for clothing. Adult moths do not feed. Damage occurs when larvae feed on wool, upholstery, rugs, felt, dried skins, hair, and similar materials. Larvae do not feed on synthetic fabrics, cotton, and other plant-based fabrics. These other fabrics may be damaged, however, if they are in contact with heavily infested fabrics made of animal fibers. You may find the larval cases in wool rugs, carpets, or stored wool clothing.

Clothes moths are small buff-colored moths with a fringe of hair along the wings and head. One species has dark spots on the wings. Female moths rarely fly and, unlike other moths, are not attracted to lights. If you see a small moth flitting around a light source it is *not* a clothes moth. Larvae can do considerable damage to certain types of fabrics and other natural articles. Generally,

Above: **clothes moth** (about ½ inch long). Notice the fringe of hairs on the head and wings. Reproduced in color on Plate 11. Modified from Ken Gray Collection, courtesy of Oregon State University (# G173-36).
Above right: **clothes moth larval cases**. Modified from Ken Gray Collection, courtesy of Oregon State University (#G174-15).
Right: **clothes moth damage to wool carpet**. Notice how the wool has been eaten away leaving behind the jute backing. Jute is made from plant fibers, which clothes moth larvae won't eat. Photo by E. A. DeAngelis. Reproduced in color on Plate 11.

only items in long-term storage, or those that are not disturbed for long periods, sustain damage. Items that are regularly used and cleaned are much less likely to be infested. Areas of wool rugs that are not vacuumed, for whatever reason, are more likely to sustain damage, too.

Clothes moth larvae cannot survive on clean fabrics. Let me repeat that: *clothes moth larvae cannot survive on clean fabrics.* Clean fabrics lack certain nutrients that larvae need, while fabrics that are soiled with dust, food, or even sweat contain these essential nutrients. The lesson here is that clean fabrics are far less likely to be infested than soiled fabrics. Always launder or dry-clean clothes before putting them into long-term storage. Use only airtight storage boxes or bags for long-term storage, and store only clean clothes. Infested closets and drawers should be emptied and thoroughly cleaned, along with their contents. *There is no need to treat indoor spaces with insecticide.* Wool wall hangings can be dry-cleaned occasionally and vacuumed as well.

Bed bug feeding (3.5x). Adult bugs are about ¼" long.

See page 20.

Fleas (Siphonaptera)

Right: **biting flea**. Head of flea is to the left.

Below: **flea larva**. This stage does not bite and is dependent on adult fleas for food.

See page 27.

Plate 2

Human lice (Anoplura)

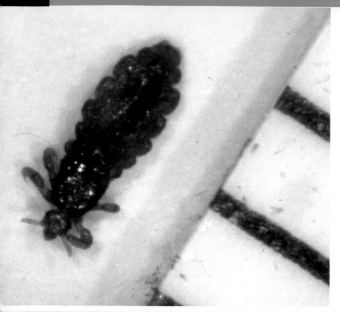

Left: **head louse**
(~ 2 mm = 1/10", rule marks
= 1 mm).This louse was
combed from hair and placed
in a preservative (alcohol)
for study. The preservative
darkened the specimen
which when alive was light
tan in color. See page 31.

Below: **pubic (crab) louse**.
The overall body shape
resembles that of a crab,
which accounts for the
vernacular name for a pubic
lice infestation—crabs.
This specimen is grasping
a hair with its large claws.
The red color at the tip of
the abdomen is recently
consumed blood that is
being excreted. See page 31.

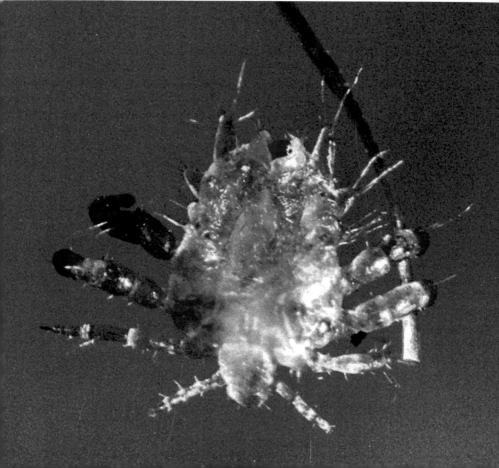

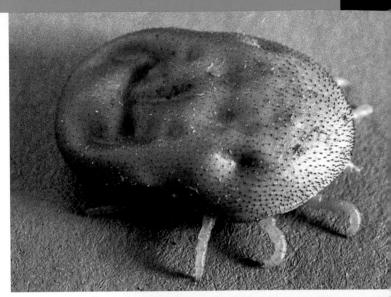

Above: **spinose ear tick**
(~0.37"), a type of soft tick. Notice
that the head of this soft tick is *not
visible* from above (compare to picture
of American dog tick, a hard tick, in
which the head is visible from above).
See page 42.

Right: **unfed hard tick**
(*Dermacentor albipictus*) (~0.18").
See page 42.

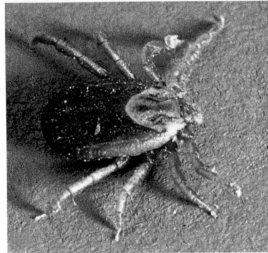

Below: **fed (engorged) hard tick**,
probably American dog tick (about ¼"
long). This tick had completed feeding
and was in the process of detaching
from our dog when it was found.
Engorged hard ticks can sometimes
be mistaken for soft ticks.
See page 42.

Plate
4

Carpenter ants (*Camponotus spp.*)

Carpenter ants.

The large ant (above, about ½" long) is a **worker** that gathers food and builds and defends the nest.

The winged ant (below, about ½–⅝" long) is a **queen**, responsible for starting new colonies and laying all the eggs.

See page 46.

Horntail wood wasps (Siricidae)

Horntail wood wasp (~1.75"). These large but harmless wasps sometimes emerge from framing lumber in recently built homes. Note the large but harmless "stinger" extending from the tail end (left).

See page 54.

Above: **Subterranean termite worker** (~0.25"). Notice how delicate this termite worker is. These worker termites are not adapted to exist outside the protected climate of the colony. See page 61.

Right: **Subterranean termite shelter tube, or "mud tube"** (on laboratory glassware). These tubes are constructed whenever termite workers move outside the colony. The presence of shelter tubes on above-ground structures can be used to detect a colony that is hidden below ground. See page 61.

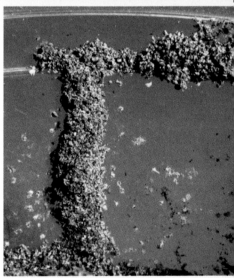

Below: **dampwood termite, winged reproductive** (~0.75–1.0"). This termite species is much larger and heavier than subterranean termites. See page 59.

Plate 6

Fire ants and harvester ants (Formicidae)

Above: **harvester ant mound**, eastern Oregon. These large, flat mounds are common in deserts, where rainfall is low and soils are gravelly. Harvester ants are red ants that forage on seeds, and vegetation is often cleared from around mounds, as in this photo. Standing or sitting on a mound of this type would be very dangerous! See page 68.

Left: **fire ant mounds** in a pasture. Individual mounds can reach 18" in height. See page 66.

Social wasps (yellowjackets, paper wasps, hornets)

Far left: **European paper wasp** (*Polistes dominulus*). Notice how similar this paper wasp is to the yellowjacket.

Left: **European paper wasp nests**, built under the flap of a trashcan liner. Notice how individual cells are visible, not enclosed in a paper envelope as they are in yellowjacket nests.

See page 74.

Above: **yellowjacket (Vespidae) wasp** (~0.5"). The biggest difference between paper wasps and yellowjacket wasps can be seen in this photograph. *The hind legs of yellowjacket wasps are short* compared to those of paper wasps, which tend to hang down in flight.

Right: Large, papery **yellowjacket nest.** Notice how the cells are not visible—they are completely enclosed in the papery envelope. Compare the yellowjacket wasp nest to photos of paper wasp nests, which have an open architecture, with the cells exposed.

Below: **Colorful yellowjacket nest.** Notice how the paper nest is similar in color to the surrounding wood that was used to make the nest paper.

See page 70.

Plate 8

Beetles (Coleoptera)

Above: **grain beetles** infesting whole grain. Notice the toothed area behind the head of each beetle, which is characteristic in this species. See page 84.

Left: **cigarette beetle larva,** *Lasioderma serricorne* (~ 0.25"). This beetle is related to the anobiid beetles that infest softwoods (see chapter 2).

Below: close-up of **carpet beetle (Dermestidae) larva** (~0.16"). Notice how fuzzy this larva appears in comparison with the larva of the cigarette beetle, which belongs to a different family. See page 82.

Above: **American cockroach nymph**, aka palmetto bug, *Periplaneta americana* (~1.0" excluding antennae). This is the largest cockroach that infests homes in the US.

Right: **German cockroach** (*Blattella germanica*). This roach is relatively easy to recognize because of the two dark strips behind the head.

Below: **cockroach egg cases** (each about ~0.2"). These single cases contain many individual eggs. Some cockroach species can be identified based on egg cases alone.

See page 85.

Plate 10

Meal or pantry moths (Lepidoptera)

Left: **Indian meal moth** (*Plodia interpunctella*). Note the dark, coppery band across the wings. Adult moths are about ⅝" across the wings.

Below: **Indian meal moth larva.** Notice the frass and webbing on raisin.

See page 90.

Carpet beetles (Dermestidae)

Left: **black carpet beetle,** *Attagenus unicolor*, (~0.20").

Below: **carpet beetle larva**. Notice the long fuzzy "tails."

See page 93.

Above: **clothes moth** (about ½" long). Notice the fringe of hairs on the head and wings.

Right: **clothes moth larval cases**.

Below: **clothes moth damage to wool carpet**. Notice how the wool has been eaten away leaving behind the jute backing. Jute is made from plant fibers, which clothes moth larvae won't eat.

See page 95.

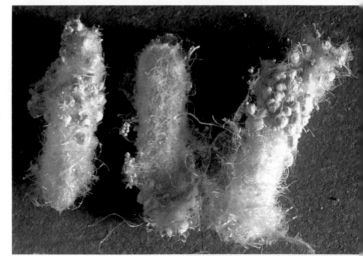

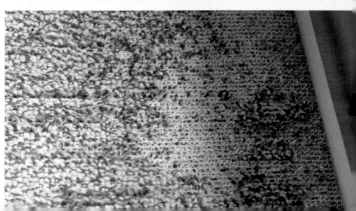

Plate 12

Horse and deer flies (Tabanidae)

Left: **deer fly** (~0.35"). Notice the multicolor pattern on the eyes. Notice also that the deer fly pictured here is about half the size of the horse fly

Below: **horse fly** (~0.70").

See page 105.

Stable flies (*Stomoxys calcitrans*)

Stable fly. Size and coloration of this fly is very similar to the common house fly. See page 106.

Above: **house fly larva** (~0.25"). Mouth and head is to the right. The "eyes," to the left, are really special organs that the larva uses to breath.

Right: **house fly pupae** (~0.25"). Fly larvae transform (metamorphose) into adult flies inside these chestnut-brown cases.

Below: **house fly** (~0.25"). Notice dark stripes behind head.

See page 114.

Plate 14

Cluster flies (*Pollenia rudis*)

Cluster fly. About ¼" long. Notice the golden scales behind head. These scales are easily rubbed off so may not be visible on all specimens.

See page 112.

Boxelder bugs *(Boisea trivittatus)*

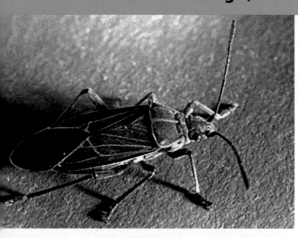

Boxelder bug (about ½" long). Notice the red marks against the dark gray or black wings.

See page 110.

Moth or drain flies (Psychodidae)

Moth or drain fly (~0.14"). Notice the hairy scales that make this fly look like a tiny moth.

See page 118.

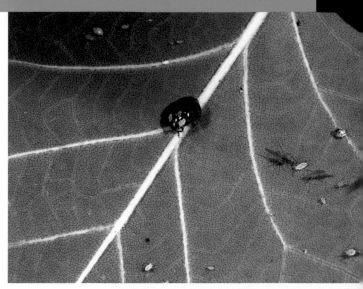

A lady beetle. While the lady beetle pictured here is not the multicolored Asian lady beetle, but a related species, it is very similar in size, shape, and even coloration. The "multicolored" part of the name refers to the many different color patterns that occur in this species.

See page 120.

Silverfish and firebrats (Lepismatidae)

Above: **silverfish** (~0.33", excluding antennae and bristletails). The head and antennae are to the *right* in this photo. The common name silverfish comes from this insect's silvery body color and fish-like scales. Silverfish are, in fact, sometimes called fishmoths. See page 121.

Below: **firebrat** (about the same size as silverfish). The head and antennae are to the *left* in this photo. Notice the three "bristletails" to the left. Firebrats are sometimes called bristletails and generally lack the silvery scales of silverfish. See page 121.

Plate 16

Vinegar flies (aka "fruit flies" or pomace flies)

Vinegar fly (~0.20"). Notice the prominent red eyes, which are characteristic of these tiny flies. See page 123.

Widow spiders (*Latrodectus spp.*)

Left: **black widow spider**. Notice the red hourglass shape on her abdomen. These markings are characteristic of widow spiders, though the markings are not always exactly this shape. Notice also the egg sac above her and the prey (probably a yellowjacket wasp), partially wrapped in silk, below her.

Below: newly hatched **widow spiderlings and egg sac.**

See page 131.

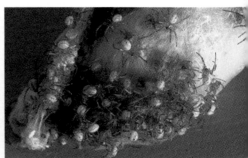

Mothballs (see chapter 12) are made of a white crystal with a strong chemical odor. They are so named because they were once used literally to fumigate closets and other clothes-storage containers for clothes moth and carpet beetles. Unfortunately, recent studies have shown that the chemicals used in mothballs are dangerous to us as well. Because we now understand the relationship between clothes moths and the cleaning of fabrics, mothballs are no longer needed and *should not be used in homes*. Mothballs were once used heavily in certain types of museums, because they protected animal and fabric specimens from insect damage. Use of mothballs is no longer permitted in most museums, however, because of the hazard they pose to workers and visitors. But even though mothballs have been removed, the distinctive odor of once-used mothballs is still present in many museums today.

Internet resources:

www.livingwithbugs.com/clothes_moth.html

Chapter 6
Tiny microscopic biting mites

People sometimes report being bitten without having seen anything that could have bitten them. Often this is a case of mistaken
identity or their imagination going haywire (chapter 11), and
sometimes the sensation is caused by an inanimate object, such
as dust or metal filings. But sometimes these bites are real. This
chapter discusses several tiny mites that bite people. The bites can
be painful and result in intense skin irritation. For the most part
the mites are so small that they are able to go unseen.

Mites are small eight-legged arthropods. A few can be larger,
such as some engorged ticks, and a few have fewer than eight legs.
Mites resemble tiny spiders in some ways. But whereas spiders
are all predators, some mites (spider mites, for example) feed on
plants, others are predators, and still others are parasites on other
animals. Ticks are covered in another chapter (chapter 1) but in
this chapter I'll discuss a few mites that bite people and cause
intensely itchy lesions. With one exception, scabies mites, *we are
not the mite's primary host*—we get bitten because we are in the
wrong place at the wrong time.

Bird and rodent nest mites (Acari)

The role of nest mites in natural ecosystems: Nest mites are ectoparasites of rodents and birds, and feed on their blood.

Every once in a while, I'm contacted by someone complaining

they are being bitten by an unseen "bug." Upon careful analysis, these skin conditions often turn out to be caused by an allergy, a reaction to some other environmental irritant, or they are entirely imaginary (chapter 11). Sometimes, however, we find a real culprit. The usual scenario is that someone wakes up in the morning with bites that look like mosquito bites. Less often, the bites occur on someone who regularly handles domesticated birds or poultry.

There are a number of parasitic mites that normally infest birds and rodents but will bite people if given the chance, or if the mites are deprived of their normal hosts. These mites normally live in the nests of their bird or rodent hosts and are sometimes called **nest mites**. If the animal nests are disturbed, or the host leaves (as when birds leave the nest to migrate at the end of summer), mites may themselves migrate in search of a new host. If they happen to enter the home and encounter you, sleeping peacefully in your bed, they will bite. Since humans are not a preferred host, the mites generally move on, leaving behind an itchy bite but no lasting damage.

Nest mites are tiny (1/32"), fast moving, and usually amber to dark gray in color. If you look at them under magnification they resemble tiny hard ticks (chapter 1). Most of the time you won't see the mites themselves unless you catch one biting you. Bites can be painless at first, and then itchy, but sometimes you'll feel a sharp stab. These bites can sometimes be mistaken for flea bites.

The first thing to do is find the source of the mites. This usually turns out to be a nearby **abandoned nest**. Rodent nests can be in walls or floors, while bird nests are usually outside near a window or vent, or in the attic. In one recent case, the birds had built a nest on the underside of the roof in a car port. Nest mites literally rained down on the cars until the nest was discovered and removed. Once you find the nest, you can remove and discard it, but *do not disturb occupied nests of song birds or birds of prey, because these birds are protected by federal laws.* Often this is enough to solve the problem. Some people resort to **fogging** with total-release aerosol insecticides to rid a room of nest mites; these

Do total-release aerosol insecticides ("bombs") work?

Not really. Total-release aerosol "bombs" are those cans of insecticide, often marketed for flea control, that, once activated, spray their contents into the air and supposedly **fog** or **fumigate** every nook and cranny of the room. In fact, these aerosols do a poor job of applying insecticide because essentially they throw large droplets into the air which then come back down, landing only on exposed surfaces. Anything that is in the shadow of furniture, etc., does not get treated. Don't waste money on these aerosols. If insecticide sprays are occasionally needed—for example, applying IGRs for flea control (chapter 1)—use a hand pump–type spray bottle instead.

"bombs" are seldom needed or even very effective, however.

Nest mites will usually go away on their own and no treatment is needed. A persistent infestation probably means there is still a nest somewhere nearby. Bites can be treated with over-the-counter ointments.

Internet resources:

www.ohioline.osu.edu/hyg-fact/2000/2101.html

Chigger mites (*Trombicula spp.*)

The role of chigger mites in natural ecosystems: Larval chigger mites are ectoparasites of mammals, including us. Later stages of this mite are predators.

Here's the scenario: you have spent the day working in your garden or hiking through brushy areas off the beaten path. That night you start to itch and develop a rash around your waist and ankles. As time goes on, the itch becomes intense and the rash worsens. You may have stumbled on **chigger mites** during the day; now they are busily feeding on your skin and injecting saliva into the wounds, causing your skin to react badly to the invasion.

Chiggers are so small (0.2–0.4 mm ~ $\frac{1}{100}$") that you probably won't see the mites themselves—but you'll sure see the results of their bites.

Chigger mites are the larval (six-legged) stage of a mite in the family Trombiculidae. They can be red, yellow, or orange in color. When seen, chiggers look like tiny red specks moving rapidly over the skin. Later stages of this mite have eight legs and do not bite. But the larvae bite humans, other mammals, reptiles, amphibians, and birds. Unlike scabies mites (see later this chapter), chiggers do not burrow into skin; instead they inject their saliva into the wound, which causes an allergic reaction and an intensely itchy area, followed by dermatitis.

Chiggers are more common in tropical or semi-tropical climates, but they occur worldwide. Some species are responsible for the transmission of scrub typhus, but not those in the US. Chigger mites can be encountered in any dense, brushy vegetation during any month in the southern US and from late spring through early fall in the northern US.

By the time the itching starts, the chigger mites may be long gone. However, since chiggers may feed for hours, or even days, taking a warm shower once bites are noticed may disrupt further feeding by washing away any remaining mites. Severe allergic

Permethrin-treated fabrics repel biting pests

Permethrin is a widely used insecticide. It is used by farmers for agricultural pests, as well as by homeowners for general outdoor pest control. Certain formulations can also be used to treat clothing and outdoor fabric gear to repel biting pests like mosquitoes, black flies, biting midges, ticks, and chiggers. The use of permethrin in this way was developed by the military and has moved into the civilian market. Once applied, the permethrin treatment lasts for weeks, through a number of washings. *Do not treat skin with permethrin.* Certain flea and tick medications for dogs contain permethrin as well. *Permethrin is toxic to cats.*

reactions should be seen by a medical professional. Less severe reactions can be treated with skincare ointments that are available over-the-counter. It is not practical to try to control either adults or larval stages of this mite with insecticide. In areas where chigger bites have occurred, the best defense is to use repellents containing DEET (chapter 1) or to treat clothing with a permethrin-based spray.

Internet resources:

www.livingwithbugs.com/chigger.html
www.livingwithbugs.com/permethr.html

Scabies and mange mites (*Sarcoptes scabei*)

The role of scabies and mange mites in natural ecosystems: These mites are ectoparasites of mammals, including us.

Next to the irritation and itch caused by the toxic oils of the poison oak and poison ivy plants, scabies probably causes the most intense and maddening itch. Unlike poison oak or ivy, however, scabies is contagious and easily passed from one person to another. Scabies is a skin ailment caused by a tiny (0.2–0.4 mm ~ $\frac{1}{100}$–$\frac{1}{50}$") mite that *burrows into the skin,* causing an allergic reaction and intense itching. The mite makes small, open sores and linear burrows just under the skin surface. Animal forms of the ailment, called **sarcoptic mange**, are caused by the same mite but there is only a small chance of crossover between, say, dog mange and human scabies. In other words, you are probably not going to contract scabies from your dog.

Human scabies occurs worldwide in all groups without regard to class or economic status—*anyone can get scabies.* Scabies outbreaks are common in overcrowded conditions such as prisons, refugee camps, and the like, which is why there is a tendency to mistakenly associate scabies only with poverty. While scabies mites do not transmit diseases, their importance is related to the skin lesions and scarring they can cause.

All stages of the mite live within burrows just under the skin's surface. Therefore treatment usually involves **medicated lotions** applied to the skin. *Repellents are not effective against scabies mites.* Scabies mites don't live long away from their host, so treatment of bedding and other household articles is generally not needed. However, bedding and clothing should be laundered in hot water. Suspected infestations should be examined by a dermatologist, since there are a number of skin conditions that resemble scabies. There are no effective treatments other than medicated skin ointments which are available by prescription only, so you'll need to see your healthcare provider.

Mange is a general term for several skin ailments caused by tiny mites that infest skin or hair follicles of dogs, cats, and other mammals. Mange mites cause an allergic reaction and intense itching. Most commonly the term is used to describe the condition caused by the sarcoptic mange mite, *Sarcoptes scabei*. This is the same mite that causes scabies in humans.

The other common mange is caused by the follicle mite *Demodex sp.* Normally this tiny mite lives in hair follicles and causes no symptoms. Occasionally, however, populations explode, causing hair loss and itching. **Demodectic mange** (demodextic mange) is often associated with stress, or other illness, which predisposes the animal to an outbreak. Mange in any form is a very serious condition and should be treated. The stress brought on by the intense itching and the secondary bacterial infections caused by wounds opened by scratching can be fatal to pets. Never allow infested animals to come into contact with uninfested animals prior to treatment.

Suspected infestations should be checked by a veterinarian, since these symptoms can be confused with other, sometimes serious diseases. Very effective treatments are now available for sarcoptic mange. Demodectic mange is often self-limiting once the causes of stress or illness are addressed. Again, however, persistent infestations associated with a foul odor resulting from a bacterial infection, and accompanied by intense itching, should be seen by a veterinarian.

Internet resources:

www.livingwithbugs.com/mange.html (mange mites in animals)
www.livingwithbugs.com/scabies.html (scabies mites in humans)

Chapter 7
Large flies that bite people and livestock

Scientists separate the thousands of different fly species into two groups, the **primitive flies** and the **higher flies**. Primitive flies are generally small and somewhat delicate (mosquitoes, midges, and gnats, for example), while higher flies are generally larger and heavier, such as house flies. Both groups are true flies and share many characteristics. And, both groups have members that feed on the blood of mammals, including mosquitoes, biting midges, black flies, horse and deer flies, and stable flies. In this chapter I'll discuss a few large-bodied higher flies that bite people and livestock—and other animals as well—to obtain blood. These flies can be extremely annoying and debilitating to livestock, but in general they don't pose the same level of threat for transmitting disease as some of the primitive flies, such as mosquitoes.

Horse and deer flies (Tabanidae)

The role of tabanid flies in natural ecosystems: The adult flies are ectoparasites of mammals; they use keen eyesight to find their host animals. Larvae (maggots) are predators that live in damp soil.

Have you have ever experienced a large fly buzzing around your head that just won't go away, no matter how much you swat at it? You might even succeed in knocking it to the ground, but still it recovers and continues annoying you. This was likely

Left: **deer fly** (~0.35"). Notice the multicolor pattern on the eyes. Notice also that the deer fly pictured here is about half the size of the horse fly. Reproduced in color on Plate 12. Modified from Ken Gray Collection, courtesy of Oregon State University (#226-5). Right: **horse fly** (~0.70"). Reproduced in color on Plate 12. Modified from Ken Gray Collection, courtesy of Oregon State University (#351-8).

a **horse fly** or **deer fly**. These large flies are common in summer around bodies of fresh water such as streams and lakes.

Horse and deer flies are large flies that bite, often painfully. They bite people as well as livestock and wildlife. Horse flies are dark in color, often appearing almost black, while deer flies are somewhat smaller and more colorful. Both have very large, prominent eyes which they use in hunting for animal hosts. Both can be very persistent and annoying when encountered. They are also relatively strong fliers. At least in the US, tabanid flies do not transmit diseases to people.

Horse flies are more likely to attack livestock, including horses, where their persistent biting can adversely affect the health of the animal. Humans are generally bothered more by deer flies, but horse flies will attack us as well. Both flies are active during daylight hours. Larvae of these flies develop in the moist soil around bodies of freshwater, so adults tend to occur near water. Adults are strong fliers, however, so they may be found some distance from their breeding grounds.

It is almost impossible to treat the soil around freshwater sources where horse and deer fly larvae live, so the best approach is to trap and repel adult flies before they bite. Both repellents containing DEET (chapter 1) and permethrin-based fabric sprays (chapter 6) work well for these annoying flies.

Traps are the best approach for protecting livestock and

horses from the annoying bites of these flies. Horse flies are highly attracted to dark objects, as these mimic a large animal in silhouette. Flies will fly toward a dark object and attempt to land on it. There are a number of non-insecticidal trap designs that incorporate various dark, three-dimensional shapes that attract and capture these flies. One simple design uses a black ball suspended below a tent that has a trap at the top. Since all flies tend to fly upward as they leave a perch, flies are captured in the trap when they fly off the dark ball, disappointed that it has not provided a good meal.

Internet resources:

www.livingwithbugs.com/horse_fl.html

Stable flies (*Stomoxys calcitrans*)

The role of stable flies in natural ecosystems: Like horse and deer flies, stable flies are ectoparasites of mammals. Stable fly larvae, however, live in decomposing vegetable matter and manure, like other manure flies.

Stable flies closely resemble the common house fly—except they bite people and livestock, sometimes painfully. Stable flies can be common pests around livestock pens and similar places where animals are boarded. Stable fly larvae, or maggots, develop in decaying vegetable matter such as straw, especially if it is mixed

Left: **stable fly.** Size and coloration of this fly is very similar to the common house fly. Reproduced in color on Plate 12. Modified from Ken Gray Collection, courtesy of Oregon State University (#G168-17).

with manure. Adult flies bite in order to feed on blood. They possess very sharp, dagger-like mouthparts which they use to pierce skin or hide. They typically feed around the lower legs of their animal hosts. Stable flies can be so annoying to livestock that they affect milk and meat production as well as weight gain.

As is true of other flies, the best way to manage stable flies is to **eliminate the breeding source**, which in this case is piles of decaying and cold-composting vegetable matter and manure. Compost piles that contain manure should be frequently turned or mixed, so that they heat up and discourage fly development. In other words, proper manure management will generally minimize problems with stable flies. Insecticides applied to facilities or the animals themselves can be effective, too, but the first step should always be proper manure management.

At times it won't be possible to manage manure well enough to get adequate control of stable, house, and face flies (another

Cold compost versus hot compost

Composting is an excellent way to get rid of excessive organic wastes such as bedding straw and vegetable matter from the kitchen and garden, as well as green manure. Composting is basically a process that encourages microbes, or bacteria and fungi, to decompose the organic material. The resulting organic *humus* is a valuable soil amendment.

Compost piles generate heat under some conditions because of a rapid decomposition process. These piles may become so hot that insects like fly larvae cannot survive in them. Some piles, however, remain cold and these serve as excellent, organically rich, breeding grounds for flies and other pests. The difference between cold and hot compost piles is usually related to their moisture content and how often they are turned or mixed. Turning allows air to reach all parts of the pile and greatly accelerates decomposition, and decomposition = heat. Piles that are too wet tend to mat together, which slows decomposition.

species of manure-breeding fly). Another option is to use **mass-reared fly parasites**. You can actually purchase these tiny parasitic wasps that attack fly pupae in manure and kill them. The parasites look like tiny winged ants. These fly parasites are often mistakenly called fly predators, so google both terms to find more information.

Internet resources:

www.livingwithbugs.com/compost.html (insects and composting)
www.edis.ifas.ufl.edu/IG133 (stable fly)

Chapter 8
Insects that invade homes but cause little damage

Certain insects seem to really annoy people. Insects that bite or sting get our attention, of course, and so do those that eat our home, such as termites or carpenter ants. But the ones that *really* get under our skin, so to speak, are the ones that come into our homes uninvited, often in large numbers, and just seem to hang around mocking us. Even though they do little or no damage, *we just want them gone.* Every year the most desperate pleas I receive usually come from homeowners dealing with one of the following unwelcome house guests. Boxelder bugs are right at the top of the list.

Boxelder bugs *(Boisea trivittatus)*

The role of boxelder bugs in natural ecosystems: Larvae feed on the leaves of maple trees.

If you're not familiar with the boxelder bug, sometimes mistakenly called boxelder *beetle,* consider yourself lucky. Even though they are harmless, these insects cause more concern among some homeowners than just about any other insect, except maybe cockroaches. When I worked for Extension, the most excited calls were almost always about boxelder bugs.

Boxelder bugs, sometimes also called **maple bugs**, are

Boxelder bug (about ½" long). Notice the red marks against the dark gray or black wings. Reproduced in color on Plate 14. Modified from Ken Gray Collection, courtesy of Oregon State University (#G167-9)

medium-sized insects about 13 mm (½") long, dark gray with red markings on their back. There is only one generation of boxelder bugs each year. Eggs are laid on maple tree leaves (boxelder is a type of maple) in early summer, and young boxelder bug nymphs develop over the next several months. The feeding nymphs do not usually harm the trees. Young bugs resemble adults except they are smaller, move more rapidly, are more red in color, and, of course, lack wings.

Autumn is when things get interesting. In the fall, after the nymphs have matured into winged adults, boxelder bugs leave the maple trees in search of protected places to spend the upcoming winter months. Their normal behavior is to find a dry crevice in the bark of a large tree, or similar protected spot, and settle down for winter. Because they tend to migrate in groups, large numbers of these bugs can congregate on trees and houses that are near the overwintering trees. As you might imagine, hundreds of relatively large bugs hanging out on the side of their house can cause a *great deal of concern* to any affected homeowner. The bugs are harmless but can be a real nuisance because of their sheer numbers. In spring the adults fly off to find maple trees on which to lay eggs. *Eggs are not laid on houses, inside or out.*

For some unfortunate homeowners, boxelder bugs are a yearly ordeal. They may even find ways to get from the siding into the house and be a nuisance all winter. If they get indoors they can soil interior furnishings with their droppings.

While it is not entirely clear why some houses are selected, boxelder bugs seem to be attracted to those that share certain characteristics. Taller buildings, two stories or higher, get more attention from these critters. So do houses that are sited high in relation to their surroundings. Boxelder bugs also favor houses with large trees immediately adjacent to them, especially if these trees are on the side that gets afternoon sun. These large trees seem to act as beacons when the adult bugs are on the move. During sunny afternoons, bugs that are resting in the trees fly onto the warm house siding.

What should a homeowner do? The first thing to do is make sure you *keep the bugs outside*. Seal around window and door frames with caulk as best you can, and put screens over vent openings. This will prevent bugs that land on the siding from finding an easy way into the house. Any bugs that do manage to find a way into living spaces can be vacuumed up and discarded. Secondly, when bugs are congregating on siding in the fall, you can treat those surfaces with a low-toxicity botanical insecticide (chapter 12) that will discourage the bugs from landing.

Internet resources:

www.livingwithbugs.com/boxelder.html

Cluster flies (*Pollenia rudis*)

The role of cluster flies in natural ecosystems: The larvae of cluster flies are endoparasites of earthworms.

Cluster flies are often described by homeowners as "*house flies that don't act right*." Cluster flies look like house flies, except for some golden scales behind the head, but this is where the similarity ends. Like boxelder bugs, cluster flies enter homes during the fall and become a nuisance. These flies cause no damage; they are not attracted to open food like house flies; and *they will not*

Cluster fly. About ¼" long. Notice the golden scales behind head. These scales are easily rubbed off so may not be visible on all specimens. Reproduced in color on Plate 14. Modified from Ken Gray Collection, courtesy of Oregon State University (#366-25)

reproduce indoors. Nevertheless, the mere presence of numerous flies inside the home is a real distraction, to say the least, for most people. I remember one distraught caller who, it turned out, had hundreds of cluster flies on her dining room ceiling and a dinner party planned for that night. House flies, on the other hand, generally won't enter homes in large numbers unless conditions inside are especially unsanitary.

Unlike other similar-looking flies, cluster flies do *not* develop in manure or garbage; they are **parasites of earthworms**. The flies actually develop inside earthworms, though they do not kill the worms. Since the flies need earthworms, they tend to be more of a nuisance in homes surrounded by turf and lawns that support healthy numbers of earthworms—pastures, golf courses, well-managed lawns, and cemeteries, for example. Cluster flies apparently do not harm earthworm populations.

Flies emerge from their earthworm hosts in the fall and

Parasite or *parasitoid*?

A **parasite** is an organism that lives off another organism, called the **host**. A **parasitoid** is a parasite that lives on, or in, the host and **ultimately kills it**. Most often the term parasitoid is used to describe an insect that parasitizes another organism by developing its young **inside the host's body**. The host is killed when the parasite emerges (think of the movie *Alien*). Cluster flies are therefore earthworm parasites, not parasitoids, because they don't kill their host.

congregate, often in large numbers, on nearby homes, seeking protected places to spend the winter months. Flies that get into wall voids and attic spaces can be a nuisance all winter long if they move into the living space. Control efforts should concentrate first on preventing flies from entering homes in the fall, and secondly on controlling any that do get in. *Do not attempt to control earthworms*, as this may actually damage the soil and turf.

First, exclude flies by repairing window screens and soffit vents, and sealing cracks around windows and doors with caulk. Even a small opening can allow flies to enter the home. These efforts will also exclude boxelder bugs and make the house generally more energy efficient and comfortable. Flies congregate on siding and may find their way into the voids between exterior wall studs. These spaces can be dusted with borates, silica, or a botanical dust insecticide (chapter 12) if you find flies entering the interior living space through wall sockets and light switches (which provide a good indication that flies are present in wall voids). Wall void treatments can be tricky; they usually involve drilling holes from the outside, similar to treatments for carpenter ants. This application can be done by a pest-control operator if you are not able to do it yourself.

Internet resources:

www.livingwithbugs.com/cluster.html

House flies (*Musca domestica*)

The role of manure flies (house flies, stable flies, and similar flies that breed in decomposing animal and vegetable matter) in natural ecosystems: Manure fly larvae live in and help break down animal and vegetable wastes, greatly accelerating decomposition.

House flies are one of the most familiar insects—and one of the most common nuisance pests around homes. There are, however, a number of other, similar-looking flies that may become a problem as well. The little house fly, *Fannia spp.*; the stable fly (chapter 7), *Stomoxys calcitrans*; and the cluster fly, *Pollenia rudis*; can all become a nuisance under some circumstances. All these flies, with the exception of the cluster fly, **breed in compost, manure, excrement, or garbage.**

House flies, sometimes called manure flies, breed in all types of animal excrement (manure), as well as in rotting meat and vegetable matter. They are most often associated with barns, stables, and kennels—anywhere animals are quartered—and garbage containers.

Small, pearly white eggs are laid on manure or garbage. Eggs hatch in a few days into larvae, or maggots. Maggots are legless, and white to yellowish in color. Fly maggots develop through three instars, becoming larger at each molt. The final instar, or prepupa, typically moves away from the garbage or manure source before pupating. Thus pupae may be found some distance from the source of flies. Adult flies live several weeks and each female fly can produce hundreds of eggs.

The presence of a few house flies is common, and no reason for concern. Large numbers of flies, however, should alert you to find the source. Look for breeding sites—such as garbage and manure, where larvae develop—and eliminate these sources before resorting to insecticides. The best way to control house flies, and other manure and garbage-breeding flies, is to locate and **eliminate the breeding source.** This may involve improving manure management or relocating garbage dumpsters. Treating these sources with pesticides is usually impractical and not very effective.

One common mistake that restaurants and other food-handling facilities make is to locate dumpsters near an outside door, through which flies originating in the garbage can easily enter the building. Another commonly overlooked source of flies is dog, or other pet, feces. Be sure to clean pet quarters frequently and dispose of feces in a *closed* garbage container.

Fly traps are sometimes useful where large numbers of flies

Above: **house fly larva** (~0.25"). Mouth and head is to the right. The "eyes," to the left, are really special organs that the larva uses to breath. Modified from Ken Gray Collection, courtesy of Oregon State University (#372-8). Above right: **house fly pupae** (~0.25"). Fly larvae transform (metamorphose) into adult flies inside these chestnut-brown cases. Modified from Ken Gray Collection, courtesy of Oregon State University (#372-16). Right: **house fly** (~0.25"). Notice dark stripes behind head. Modified from Ken Gray Collection, courtesy of Oregon State University (#G148-32). Reproduced in color on Plate 13.

are present outdoors, or when flies have entered a building. Traps usually consist of an attractant bait or ultraviolet light source and some type of trap container or sticky surface. Ultraviolet light traps are available for use inside food-handling facilities, restaurants, and grocery stores; these attract flies with light and kill flies that land on an electrified grid or sticky surface. Traps should be a second line of defense, *after* all attempts to reduce breeding sources have been completed.

A relatively new way to control house flies is with poison baits that contain an insecticide and attractive bait. These bait products can be used around the outside of commercial facilities and agricultural buildings to suppress fly numbers. Use of bait must be combined with proper sanitation, however.

Internet resources:

www.livingwithbugs.com/hous_fly.html

Fungus gnat larva (above) and adult fly (below). These delicate, dark-colored flies resemble small mosquitoes

Fungus gnats

The role of gnats in natural ecosystems: The larvae of gnats live in the soil, where they feed on organic debris and plant roots.

Fungus gnats are tiny, dark-colored flies whose larvae live in the soil and **feed on the roots of plants.** Fungus gnats can be pests in potted houseplants, and in greenhouses and facilities where mushrooms are grown. You may not notice a few of these tiny flies around your houseplants, but under some conditions the populations build so rapidly that clouds of these flies are stirred up whenever the plants are touched. In commercial mushroom growing houses, this pest not only reduces mushroom growth (mushrooms grow on soil much like plants) but also may be present in such quantities that workers are prevented from harvesting the crop without special equipment.

In greenhouses, fungus gnats can be monitored with yellow cards coated with a sticky material. Flies are attracted to the cards and get stuck to their surface. Counting the number of flies stuck to the traps enables measurement of the fungus gnat population.

Fungus gnat populations build rapidly when potting soils are rich in organic matter and fairly wet. The first step to reducing the number of fungus gnats is to dry out the soil as much as possible without affecting plant, or mushroom, growth. Houseplants are often overwatered. Overwatering not only hurts the plant but allows fungus gnats to thrive. Before you water your houseplants, check the soil. The top of the soil should feel dry to the touch.

Greenhouses and mushroom growers use a biorational microbial insecticide (chapter 12) to control fungus gnat larvae. Homeowners should not need to resort to insecticides to control fungus gnats if they remember to allow potting soil to dry out between waterings.

Internet resources:

www.livingwithbugs.com/fungus_gnat.html

Moth or drain flies (Psychodidae)

The role of psychodid flies in natural ecosystems: Larvae feed on bacteria and algae in semi-aquatic habitats. Some adult flies are ectoparasites (sand flies), but these parasitic species do not occur in the US.

"*I've got tiny black bugs coming out of my bathroom drain!*" I get this e-mailed query about once a month, and the senders usually think they have entered some kind of horror movie. In fact this is a common household insect and no reason for concern. The insects are indeed coming out of the drain, but they won't

Moth or drain fly (~0.14"). Notice the hairy scales that make this fly look like a tiny moth. Reproduced in color on Plate 14. Modified from Ken Gray Collection, courtesy of Oregon State University (#149-20)

A relative of moth flies that carries leishmaniasis

Leishmaniasis is a parasitic disease spread by the bite of infected **sand flies**. Sand flies belong to the same family as moth flies. *Note: these are not the same insect that is sometimes called a "sand fly" in the southeastern US, which is actually a biting midge (chapter 1).* Leishmaniasis is very rare in North America but there are several different forms of the disease throughout the world. The most common forms are **cutaneous leishmaniasis**, which causes skin sores, and **visceral leishmaniasis**, which affects some of the body's internal organs. Cutaneous leishmaniasis is common in parts of the Middle East and has received more attention in recent years because of the number of US soldiers affected while in Iraq. www.cdc.gov/NCIDOD/DPD/parasites/leishmania/factsht_leishmania.htm

bite, nor do they pose any other threat. They are called drain flies or, more correctly, **moth flies**.

Moth or drain flies are small hairy flies that develop in the organic slime that forms inside household drains, around sewage ponds and compost bins, and even in the algae mats that form sometimes around bodies of water. When the flies occur indoors, it is usually a sign that sink drains and traps need to be cleaned. The new bacterial drain cleaner treatments work well to remove this material without harsh chemicals and eliminate the place where flies develop.

Internet resources:

www.livingwithbugs.com/drain_fly.html

Multicolored Asian lady beetle (*Harmonia axyridis*)

The role of lady beetles in natural ecosystems: Both larvae and adults are predators of small prey like aphids and spider mites.

It is ironic that one of the few universally loved insects can become such a pest at times. Most people like lady beetles, or ladybugs, and they regularly make an appearance in children's stories and films. One recent story in our local newspaper showed school kids releasing lady beetles in an agricultural field as a way to learn how "good bugs" can control "bad bugs." While most lady beetles are harmless and even beneficial, one species can become a pest because of its habit of roosting in homes and outbuildings during winter.

The **multicolored Asian lady beetle** is not native to the US. It was intentionally imported a number of years ago to control aphids that feed on trees. This lady beetle has been wildly successful and has so increased in numbers that it is starting to displace native lady beetle species. Besides its success as a predator, this species has the habit of congregating in large masses in people's homes and other buildings at certain times of the year. All lady beetles congregate in the fall and spend the winter in overwintering masses. This behavior is the basis of the lady beetle industry that collects beetles to sell to gardeners. The problem is that while our native species select out-of-the-way places to roost for the winter, the multicolored Asian lady beetle prefers to spend the winter with us, in our homes. So while they serve a beneficial purpose as predators of pest aphids, they are also seen as pests themselves by some homeowners.

Like boxelder bugs and cluster flies, the best way to deal with

A lady beetle. While the lady beetle pictured here is not the multicolored Asian lady beetle, but a related species, it is very similar in size, shape, and even coloration. The "multicolored" part of the name refers to the many different color patterns that occur in this species. Reproduced in color on Plate 15. Modified from Ken Gray Collection, courtesy of Oregon State University (#G133-23)

pesky lady beetles is to prevent them from entering homes in the fall by sealing cracks around doors and windows, fixing broken screens, and screening vents. These measures have the added benefit of sealing out other pests as well as the weather. If beetles get indoors, sweep them up and deposit them outside. Some people even store them in the refrigerator for release into the garden in the spring. Give them a little water in a plastic container in the fridge. *Do not resort to insecticides*—they won't be very effective and they can also cause respiratory and other health problems when used indoors.

Internet resources:

www.livingwithbugs.com/harmonia.html

Silverfish and firebrats (Lepismatidae)

The role of lepismatids (silverfish and firebrats) in natural ecosystems: These primitive insects are scavengers that feed on plant debris.

These primitive, wingless insects can be identified by their long antennae and three long "bristletails" that project from their back end. In fact, an old common name for them is bristletails. They are ½" to ¾" long when fully grown. Silverfish are somewhat

Top: **silverfish** (~0.33", excluding antennae and bristletails). The head and antennae are to the *right* in this photo. The common name silverfish comes from this insect's silvery body color and fish-like scales. Silverfish are, in fact, sometimes called fishmoths. Modified from Ken Gray Collection, courtesy of Oregon State University (#390-17). Below: **firebrat** (about the same size as silverfish). The head and antennae are to the *left* in this photo. Notice the three "bristletails" to the left. Firebrats are sometimes called bristletails and generally lack the silvery scales of silverfish. Modified from Ken Gray Collection, courtesy of Oregon State University (#423-2). Reproduced in color on Plate 15.

Basement, crawl space, or slab construction

Homes are generally built over a basement or crawl space, or on a concrete slab. The method of construction can influence the type of insect pests you experience in your home. **Basements** are completely enclosed spaces with, usually, a concrete floor and a standard eight-foot-high ceiling. They often have windows as well. Basements can be waterproofed, and even heated, and hence tend to be somewhat drier and less hospitable to some insect pests. Dry basements also protect the underside of the first floor from water damage.

In **crawl space construction**, the house is built over bare soil that is often only a few feet or less away from the framing wood of the first floor. There are no windows in crawl space construction; instead, screened vents are added to the foundation wall to vent this space. Crawl spaces are unheated and usually damp. The bare soil of the crawl space should be covered with heavy plastic to reduce moisture. Never close the foundation vents except in the coldest months of winter. Crawl spaces are great places for **ants, termites, silverfish, spiders,** and **mice**. Because of the moisture in crawl spaces you should check the first-floor wood framing for mold and moisture damage at least once a year.

Some careless homebuilders bury wood construction debris or tree stumps in the soil of the crawl space or under concrete slabs (see below), because this is cheaper than hauling it away. Most builders would never do this—and the practice is banned in most areas—but it does happen. This buried wood can become infested with **subterranean termites** (chapter 2) which will eventually spread into the rest of the home. If you are building a home or purchasing a recently built one, be sure to ask the builder about their disposal practices.

In the third type of construction, the house (or part of it) is built on a **concrete slab**. The slab is usually insulated and waterproofed from the underlying soil, but it has holes in it for utility pipes. The concrete slab serves as the framing for the first floor, so there is no wood framing that can be damaged by moisture. If the utility holes are properly sealed, this type of construction prevents most insects from entering the home from below.

shiny and silvery-gray in color, while firebrats are dull, mottled, and gray-brown. Firebrats also have more stiff hairs along their bodies. Both insects feed on paper and starchy materials, which may lead them to damage books, stored papers, pictures, and wallpaper. They will even infest stored foodstuffs like cereal, grains, dry pet food, and dried meats.

Silverfish prefer cool, damp habitats like basements and crawl spaces, while firebrats tend to occur in hotter, drier areas like attics. Our crawl space, for example, which has a dirt floor covered with plastic sheeting, produces a regular of supply of pesky silverfish.

Control of silverfish can usually be accomplished by reducing water and moisture sources. Many times, however, you won't be able to reduce moisture sufficiently—in a crawl space, for example—and instead you'll just have to be content with protecting things in storage from these insects. Insecticide treatment, if absolutely necessary, should be restricted to uninhabited areas of the house such as attics and crawl spaces. Firebrats can be effectively managed with insecticidal dusts that are placed in dry areas where these insects are found. Remember to protect boxes of valuable books, and other paper documents, by *completely sealing storage boxes with tape.*

Internet resources:

www.livingwithbugs.com/sil_fish.html

Vinegar flies (aka "fruit flies" or pomace flies)

The role of vinegar flies in natural ecosystems: Larvae of vinegar flies live in rotting vegetable compost and feed on bacteria and fungi.

The common name **fruit fly** is used for two very different flies, unfortunately, and this causes some confusion. The small fly that you find sometimes in kitchens, around the salad bar at

Vinegar fly (~0.20").
Notice the prominent red eyes,
which are characteristic of these
tiny flies. Reproduced in color on
Plate 16. Modified from Ken Gray
Collection, courtesy of Oregon
State University (#254-27)

restaurants, or in cold-composted compost bins (chapter 7) is
the **vinegar fly**, or **pomace fly** (*Drosophila spp.*). There is also a
larger fly with ornately patterned wings that infests tree fruit and
other crops, which is properly called a fruit fly, or picture-wing
fly (Tephritidae). The most familiar example of a true fruit fly
is the Mediterranean fruit fly, or "Med fly," that occasionally
invades agricultural areas of California and Florida and does so
much damage to produce. Most people, however, including many
entomologists, refer to both these different flies as "fruit flies."

The only fly in this group that gets into homes is the vinegar
fly, or pomace fly. The word *pomace* refers to the solid remains
of fruit after it is pressed to extract juice. Vinegar flies are small,
brownish flies with distinctive **red eyes**. Fly larvae feed on the
decay fungi that grow in overripe or rotting fruit. Adult female
flies lay eggs in the skins of vegetables and fruit. The females are
attracted to the vinegar-like odor of rotting fruit, which is the
origin of one of their common names.

Vinegar flies in genetic research

It turns out that vinegar flies play an important role in research.
These flies are very easy to rear in the laboratory, as well as the
kitchen compost pail, and have served as a key model species in
genetics research for many years. You'll often see references to the
"fruit fly" when someone is talking about genetics research. *Now
you know they should be calling it a vinegar fly.*

Vinegar flies cause no direct damage to vegetables or fruit, but they can be a nuisance when present in large numbers. **Fruit fly traps** are available for use in kitchens and restaurants. These traps contain vinegar as the attractant. Proper disposal of fruit and vegetable scraps and compost is usually all that is needed to eliminate vinegar flies in restaurants. Poorly managed dumpsters are often an important source of these and other flies outdoors. Use of insecticides to control vinegar flies is generally not necessary.

Internet resources:

www.livingwithbugs.com/fruitfly.html

Chapter 9
Dust mites (*Dermatophagoides spp.*)

The role of dust mites in natural ecosystems: Dust mites are scavengers. Some feed on the skin shed by mammals, including humans.

Dust mites are tiny, almost microscopic critters that live on the organic debris that we leave behind as we move through our lives. Most people don't know that we actually shed parts of our skin every day, just as a dog sheds hair. Healthy skin is constantly renewed from below and older dead skin is shed from the top; this is how skin heals itself. The shed skin is part of the debris that accumulates in our homes that we call dust. House dust is a mixture of ash, cloth fibers, hair, plant pollen, flakes of human and animal skin (dander), soil particles, and fungal spores. In many households, human skin flakes by themselves make up much of the total volume of house dust.

House-dust mites have figured out a way to use all this organic debris as food. We might never be aware of dust mites, however, because they are so small—except that *what goes into the dust mite as a flake of skin comes out the other end as an* **allergen,** capable of causing a stuffy nose (rhinitis) or even life-threatening asthma. House dust mites are not the only source of allergens in our indoor environment, but they may be one of the most important.

As homes are sealed tighter and tighter against the elements in order to conserve energy, house-dust mites have become more of a problem. Dust-mite allergy can be managed by a combination

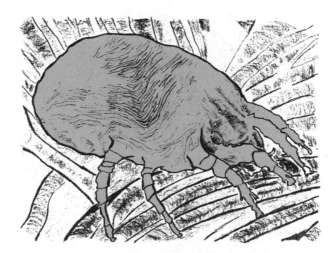

Drawing, close-up (highly magnified) of a **dust mite** on fabric

of lowering indoor humidity, controlling the allergen pool, and medically treating the allergy itself.

Dust mites are very small; you can't see them directly. Almost every house has dust mites but some houses have more than others. Dust-mite eggs develop into adults in about one month under ideal conditions. Growth in the mite population occurs between 50°F and 90°F and with a high relative humidity of between 60% and 90%. For this reason, dust mites tend to be more numerous in the spring and fall, when the humidity indoors is a little higher. Heating during the winter months tends to dry out the house and will reduce dust mite numbers. However, since windows are closed in winter, which increases indoor air pollution, allergies may actually be worse. House-dust mites do not bite or otherwise cause injury.

You should always discuss a serious allergic reaction with your physician or allergist, because these reactions can get worse over time with repeated exposure to the allergen. Tests are available to determine if dust-mite allergen is responsible. Serious allergic reactions should be treated medically. Mite numbers—and the allergen pool—can be reduced by lowering indoor humidity through either central heating or air conditioning. Also, try to control other sources of allergen such as cockroaches, fleas, and

Dust-mite allergies

An **allergic reaction**, or allergy, is a reaction by our body to a foreign protein such as plant pollen, venom, or dust mite poop (poop is the *technical term* for feces). When the body detects this foreign protein, it releases antibodies to wage a type of war against the invader. The reason the body mounts this defense is because many foreign proteins turn out to be disease-causing bacteria and viruses. The problem is that the body sometimes can't tell the difference between a harmless dust-mite allergen or pollen, on the one hand, and a potentially deadly disease pathogen, on the other—so the body overreacts.

The release of antibodies, along with a chemical called histamine, are the reasons for the symptoms of an allergy; these can range from a stuffy nose to **anaphylactic shock** and even death. Individuals differ in their tolerance, or reaction, to dust mite allergens. Some people never exhibit any allergic reaction, while in others the reaction is severe.

The ways to avoid an allergic reaction, or to lessen the symptoms, are (1) avoid contact with the allergen (the foreign proteins that elicit the reaction), (2) treat the effects of histamine with an **antihistamine** medication, or (3) become desensitized to the allergen so the body learns to react less to a particular allergen such as grass pollen or dust-mite allergen.

For dust-mite allergy sufferers, all three ways to avoid a reaction are available. You can avoid contact with the allergen by reducing dust mite numbers, proper cleaning, room air purification, and the use of allergen-proof mattress covers. Antihistamine medications are widely available to combat the effects of histamine, and "allergy shots" are available that will desensitize individuals.

silverfish. Keep pets and their dander out of the bedroom, and limit the use of natural-fiber furnishings like rugs.

General cleaning is also an effective tool against dust mites and allergen. Shampoo rugs and fabric-covered furniture and eliminate as much surface dust as possible. Remove carpets from bedrooms—wood or tile flooring is easier to clean than carpets. *Wet clean (shampoo) remaining carpets regularly.* Vacuuming alone may actually make matters worse by stirring up dry dust and allergens.

Internet resources:

www.livingwithbugs.com/dustmite.html

Chapter 10
Medically significant spiders in North America

Many, perhaps most, people are fearful of spiders because they believe that all spiders are venomous, even deadly. The fact is that while a few spiders do have a venomous (but rarely deadly) bite, most are harmless, incapable of even piercing human skin with their fangs. I know that most people are afraid of spiders, and almost nothing I could write here is going to change that, but here's some information that will hopefully put your questions about "poisonous" spiders into perspective.

Researchers often divide the world of spiders into venomous and non-venomous species. In recent years, however, studies have shown that, with a few exceptions, even those species once considered highly venomous are in reality not so dangerous, now that scientists have examined them in detail. As a result, some researchers are now using the term **medically significant** to refer to spiders whose bites may cause injury but the exact cause of the injury is not known. In other words: something "medically significant" is going on with these bites, but the details remain unknown. In the US there are only a few medically significant spiders. In this chapter

Poison or venom?

A **poison** is a toxin that is usually taken into the body through the mouth. A **venom** is a toxin that is injected directly into the bloodstream. Rattlesnakes and black widow spiders have venom, and so should be described as **venomous** rather than **poisonous**.

I'll describe the ones you are most likely to encounter and try to provide some guidance in how to avoid any such encounters.

The role of spiders in natural ecosystems: All spiders are predators; some actively hunt, while others use elaborate traps (webs) to capture prey.

Widow spiders (*Latrodectus spp.*)

Widow spiders, which are one of only a very few dangerous spiders found in the US, are among the **most venomous** spiders in the world. They achieve this distinction because their bite may contain a neurotoxic venom, or nerve poison, which can impair breathing and even, in rare cases, lead to death. Widow spider bites do not cause ulcerating wounds or infections. Unlike some other venomous spiders around the world, widow spiders are secretive and not quick to bite. Their fangs are fairly short and usually won't pierce clothing. However, since widow spiders are fairly common in the US (except for Alaska), and very common in some southern states, they are worth getting to know and learning to avoid.

Widow spiders are fairly large, with a body length of roughly ½" and a total length of about 1½". They are shiny black to brown in color with one or several red spots that are sometimes in the shape of an hourglass. Unlike some other spiders that construct elaborate, intricate webs, widow spiders make a diffuse, poorly defined web. There are a number of species of widow spiders in the US; the most familiar is probably the **black widow spider** (*Lactrodectus mactans*). The black widow spider sports the classic **red hourglass marking** on the underside against a shiny black background. These spiders occur in undisturbed areas and under debris. *They rarely bite, but their bites can be very dangerous.* Fortunately widow spider antivenom is now widely available. Be cautious when working around woodpiles or undisturbed debris in areas where widow spiders might occur. Widow spiders tend to

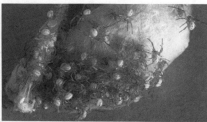
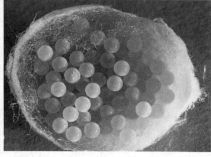

Left: **black widow spider**. Notice the red hourglass shape on her abdomen. These markings are characteristic of widow spiders, though the markings are not always exactly this shape. Notice also the egg sac above her and the prey (probably a yellowjacket wasp), partially wrapped in silk, below her. Reproduced in color on Plate 16. Modified from Ken Gray Collection, courtesy of Oregon State University (#220-16). Top right: newly hatched **widow spiderlings and egg sac.** Reproduced in color on Plate 16. Modified from Ken Gray Collection, courtesy of Oregon State University (#228-9). Below right: **spider eggs inside egg sac** (~1.0" across). Modified from Ken Gray Collection, courtesy of Oregon State University (#229-36)

be more common in dry and warm climates but occur throughout North America.

Widow spiders rarely enter the living space of houses but will construct webs in an undisturbed crawl space or outbuilding. In fact, encounters with widow spiders were far more common when people used outhouses. Nowadays the most frequent encounter occurs when people pick up boards or other yard debris. Insecticidal control of widow spiders is not needed.

Internet resources:

www.livingwithbugs.com/spiders.html
www.en.wikipedia.org/wiki/Widow_spider

Hobo spider (*Tegenaria agrestis*)

People simply do not like fast-moving, long-legged, hairy spiders. Nothing provokes a reaction like a big, hairy spider in the bathtub or kitchen sink first thing in the morning. This scenario happens so often that some people actually believe that the spiders emerge from sink drains, like drain flies (chapter 8). In fact, the spiders fall into the tubs and sinks by accident and are then trapped by the slippery walls. A few spiders enter homes from outdoors in search of prey and water. Almost all indoor spiders are small and go unnoticed, but a few are larger and get our attention when discovered. Of the large, fast moving spiders, the **house spiders** may be the most common.

Three related house spiders commonly enter homes in search of food and water. The **common house spider** (*Tegenaria domestica*), the **giant house spider** (*Tegenaria duellica*), and the **hobo spider** (*Tegenaria agrestis*). These three species are very difficult to tell apart, except for fully grown, female giant house spiders, which are considerably larger than the other two. Of the three **only the hobo spider is thought to have a dangerous bite** and even these reports may be somewhat exaggerated.

The **common house spider** is found throughout North America, while the **giant house spider** is found mainly in the Pacific Northwest and western Canada. The **hobo spider** is currently

Hobo spider = aggressive house spider

The hobo spider is sometimes called the aggressive house spider. The more accepted common name, however, is hobo spider. The name aggressive house spider comes from the species name *"agrestis"* which many people (including, unfortunately, yours truly) have mistakenly understood to mean "aggressive." In fact, "agrestis" refers to "agrarian," which means *related to land or farming*. In Europe, where this spider originated, it is commonly encountered by farmers in grain fields during harvest, hence the name "agrestis."

Left: **hobo spider**, drawing. Body length is about ½"; leg tip to leg tip is about 1½".
Above: **range map for the hobo spider in the US** (redrawn from www.washington.edu/burkemuseum/spidermyth/myths/hobo.html)

expanding its range from the Pacific Northwest, both east and south. These house spiders vary in size from about the size of a quarter (including the long legs) to about the size of a half dollar, sometimes even larger. They have long legs, are generally brown or tan in color, and are fast-moving. They can be easily confused with other spiders that occur outdoors. All three house spiders originated in Europe where, interestingly, the hobo spider is not considered to be a venomous species.

There are many reports of serious localized **necrotic wounds** (necrotic = dead flesh) resulting from hobo spider bites. Wounds begin as sore, inflamed areas around the site of the bite. These areas may eventually become open infections that are difficult to heal. People with compromised immune systems are more likely to develop these serious wounds. While it certainly appears that the spider bite and the infections are related, some researchers are starting to doubt that this spider is venomous at all; instead, they attribute the serious wounds to a **bacterial infection** that may be initiated by the spider bite. While the scientific jury may still be out, care should be taken with this common spider where it occurs. Take special care when working around woodpiles and handling firewood; wear garden gloves if possible. Encounters with all house spiders are far more common during the fall, when amorous male spiders are wandering in search of female spiders. During the rest of the year these spiders tend to be fairly secretive.

Internet resources:

www.livingwithbugs.com/hobo_spider.html

Brown recluse spider (*Loxosceles reclusa*)

The **brown recluse spider** is a seriously misunderstood critter. It is the subject of much fear and loathing, even in regions where it does not occur, and it gets blamed for wounds that probably have other causes. When I took calls from our Extension Master Gardeners in Oregon, one of the most frequent questions was about the brown recluse spider, which does not occur within hundreds of miles of Oregon. Many people, often misinformed by local news sources, were convinced that it did occur in Oregon; some claimed to have been bitten and to have a medical diagnosis. The

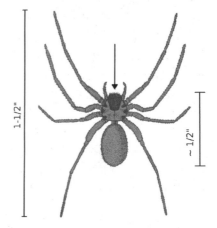

Above: **approximate distribution of brown recluse spider.** This spider is only found in the south-central US. (Modified from Vetter, R. (2004), *Causes of Necrotic Wounds other than Brown Recluse Spider Bites*, www.spiders.ucr.edu/necrotic.html).

Right: **brown recluse spider**, drawing. Body length is less than ½"; leg tip to leg tip is about 1½". Note violin-shaped mark on back (arrow). The "violin" has a thin neck and wide body. The neck of the violin is pointing backwards. Redrawn from *CDC Pictorial Keys Arthropods, Reptiles, Birds and Mammals of Public Health Significance* (US Department of Health, Education, and Welfare, Public Health Service. 1967)

Dangerous skin bacteria and spider bites

Recent studies have shown a possible link between certain **bacteria** and the ugly, open wounds that had once been diagnosed as **spider bites**. The bacterium known as MRSA (**m**ethicillin-**r**esistant *Staphylococcus aureus*) causes very severe, ulcerating infections of the skin. The infested areas are very red and tender, and in some people these infections can lead to open wounds that require surgery to heal. These are the same wound symptoms that have been associated with bites from certain spiders, most commonly the **brown recluse spider** and the **hobo spider**, in the US. The observation that led researchers to look for a cause of these severe wounds other than spider bites was how often the wounds occur in regions of the US where neither of these two spiders are naturally found.

Does this mean that brown recluse and hobo spiders are not venomous? Perhaps not. What it does mean is that the story is, like most biological stories, more complex than we thought. It could be that spider bites somehow make the bacterial infections more common or more severe. Nobody knows the complete answer yet, but fortunately the medical treatments for either type of wound are very similar.

hobo spider, which does occur in Oregon, is somewhat similar in size and color to the brown recluse spider, and probably accounts for the majority of these cases of mistaken identity. Having said this, the brown recluse is relatively large and, where it naturally occurs, has the unfortunate habit of entering homes. But the facts are these: it has a much more limited distribution than people believe, and while its bite may be venomous, it is not nearly as dangerous as the widow spiders.

Brown recluse spiders are medium-sized (20–40 mm leg span [a US quarter is about 25 mm in diameter]; body length ~10 mm), tan to brown in color, and have a very distinctive violin shape mark on the front half (cephalothorax) of the spider when viewed from above. The brown recluse spider is a hunting, wandering spider and does not use a web to capture prey. The brown recluse spider occurs *only in the south-central US* (see range map). A related species occurs as far west as California but apparently does not bite and cause wounds. *Reports of bites from outside the map area are probably misdiagnosed.* Many people, including some in the medical community, will argue with that last sentence, but it has been confirmed by scientists who study the natural range of this spider.

The brown recluse spider is often reported outside its natural range based solely on observation of wounds. Many slow-healing, necrotic wounds have been mistakenly blamed on this spider. Within its home range, however, the brown recluse spider can be very common and abundant, although authenticated bites are relatively rare. Insecticidal control of the brown recluse spider is sometimes necessary in homes (see Internet resources). Non-insecticidal traps (see below) can be useful, too, since this spider, like the hobo spider, readily moves around indoors.

Like other wandering/hunting spiders, brown recluse spiders are sometimes found associated with packing materials and shipped goods. Spiders can be accidentally transported from their natural range to other areas. For this reason, lone spiders will occasionally be found outside their home range; it is highly unlikely that these displaced spiders will survive and colonize the new area, however.

Internet resources:

www.livingwithbugs.com/recluse.html

Yellow sac spiders (*Cheiracanthium spp.*)

Yellow sac spiders are small (body length less than ½"), yellow- to tan-colored spiders. Yellow sac spider bites may cause stinging pain like those of a wasp or yellowjacket. This can be followed by redness, swelling and itching, and even an open sore. The wounds made by yellow sac spiders are subject to the same kind of skin infections that have been attributed to brown recluse and hobo spider bites. In fact, some of the bites that have been diagnosed as brown recluse and hobo spider bites, especially those reported outside the natural range of these spiders, may have been caused by one of the yellow sac spiders.

Internet resources:

www.en.wikipedia.org/wiki/Yellow_sac_spider (photograph of the yellow sac spider)

Safe ways to deal with indoor spiders

Spiders found outdoors can *always* be left alone. Spiders are beneficial because they prey on insects and other arthropods and are an important part of the natural ecosystem. They do not generally pose a threat as long as you exercise reasonable caution. Wear work gloves when working around woodpiles or debris piles. Widow spiders tend to occur in out-of-the-way places in outbuildings and crawl spaces, so be cautious in such locations as well.

Sticky board traps are usually the best solution for spiders that wander indoors, such as male hobo and recluse spiders. Widow spiders only rarely enter living spaces, and if they are found they can be individually removed.

Most spiders stay close to their webs, lying in wait for prey. Some spiders, however, wander in search of prey, or a mate, at certain times of the year. Male hobo spiders (in the fall) and recluse spiders are of this wandering type. Since wandering species move from place to place, they are more likely to be encountered by us. The number of wandering-type spiders found indoors can be reduced using sticky board traps.

Sticky board traps are made of cardboard with a sticky material coating on one surface. Traps can be placed along baseboards at the edges of rooms, where wandering spiders tend to move.

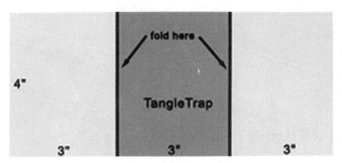

Layout for homemade spider trap. Fold along lines and tape along top to make a triangular "tube." Paint or spray the inside with Tangle-Trap Insect Trap Coating™.

Spiders get trapped when they try to cross the sticky surface. No insecticides or attractants are needed. Spider traps can be purchased or you can make your own. The simplest homemade trap is a piece of cardboard folded into a triangular tube about four inches long and three inches high. The inside bottom surface should be coated with sticky material such as Tangle-Trap Insect Trap Coating™.

To construct a simple trap cut a piece of cardboard (cereal box cardboard works great) about 4 by 9 inches. Draw lines at 3-inch intervals along the long side and paint the middle section with Tangle-Trap™ sticky coating. Tangle-Trap™ is available as an aerosol spray, a thick paste, and a brush-on liquid. Use the brush-on formula, because it is easier to apply. If the cardboard is too absorbent, coat it first with a water-based polyurethane, or use the printed side. Fold the sides up and tape along the top to make a triangular tube.

Place your traps with the long side against baseboards, behind furniture, and inside cabinets. Spiders usually travel near the base of walls or other vertical surfaces. When they encounter the trap opening, they will wander inside and get caught in the sticky material. Dispose of used or dirty traps in the trash.

Internet resources:

www.livingwithbugs.com/spider_tp.html

Chapter 11
Real and imaginary fears

Certain insects, and especially spiders, evoke fear in most people. Even entomologists and arachnologists (people who study spiders) are cautious around insects or spiders they know are dangerous. This fear is *perfectly normal* and has a survival benefit that has been honed over millions of years of human evolution—to avoid injury from venomous bites or stings. On the other hand, these fears become overwhelming for some people and limit their daily activities. For them the normal, rational fear of a potentially dangerous encounter has escalated beyond their control.

The medical community recognizes two different conditions related to the fear of real or imagined arthropods, including insects, spiders, and their close relatives, like scorpions. The first occurs when someone exhibits an overly intense, irrational fear of all arthropods, whether or not they actually pose a threat. This condition is generally called **entomophobia** (*entomo* = insect (in the broad sense), *phobia* = irrational fear). The key feature of entomophobia is that a *real* arthropod is the trigger. In other words: *the fear (or response) is irrational, but the stimulus (arthropod) is real.*

An example of entomophobia might be when someone encounters a small, harmless insect in their home and are made so fearful by this encounter that they do something irrational, such as having the house fumigated or even moving out. Even though they know the insect is harmless, their fears simply will not allow them to deal with the situation in a rational manner. If the phobia

The Dragons of Eden: Speculations on the Evolution of Human Intelligence, by Carl Sagan (1977)

Dr. Carl Sagan (1934–1996) published this classic about the origin of human intelligence and the roots of our fears over thirty years ago; the book won a Pulitzer Prize in 1978 and is still in print today. It takes the reader on a journey back in time and shows why our innate fears of things like spiders and snakes were important to our survival. Dr. Sagan speculates about the survival benefit of certain fears for our ancestors, and how these fears can become a disadvantage in the modern world. If we believe Dr. Sagan's thesis, it seems that the fears that helped our ancestors avoid dangerous animals are the same ones that lead some modern humans to an unreasonable fear of all things that creep or crawl.

involves a spider, then it could be called **arachnophobia** (*arachno* = spider). Like other phobias, entomophobia and arachnophobia can often be treated with what is called **desensitization therapy.**

Contrast entomophobia with the second, much more serious condition known as **delusory parasitosis**, or **delusions of parasitosis,** also called **Ekbom's syndrome.** A delusion is something that is imagined, and is not real. Delusory parasitosis is therefore an **imagined infestation by a parasite.** The key feature here is that the *stimulus or trigger is not real* but imagined. In this case, the person believes, wrongly, that they are infested with an insect or mite or are being bitten repeatedly. The underlying cause of the delusion can be psychiatric illness, or it can be triggered by something as simple as an allergic reaction, emotional stress, physical illness, or even recreational drug use. As with other delusional disorders, the root causes of the psychological disorder must be found and dealt with, and counseling is often needed.

In recent years, the term **Morgellons** has been used to describe a particular skin condition in which tiny thread-like bodies appear embedded in the skin. The origin of these threads is not known. Some researchers believe they are only textile fibers;

others, however, believe that Morgellons represents a new, as yet undescribed infectious disease. Still others believe that there is an association with collembola (springtails), which are small primitive insect-like arthropods that live in damp soil and feed on organic debris. Most entomologists discount the association of skin ailments with collembola, because these critters have neither the morphology nor ecology to live on human skin.

Internet resources:

www.livingwithbugs.com/del_pho.html
www.delusion.ucdavis.edu/delusional.html
www.en.wikipedia.org/wiki/Delusional_parasitosis

Chapter 12
More about pest control

Mothballs

Until fairly recently, mothballs were used to protect textiles in storage from insects that damage natural fabrics (chapter 5). The use of mothballs was so widespread that the verb to mothball is synonymous with putting something into storage or taking something out of service (as in: "mothballing the old machinery"). However, nowadays we are realizing that the chemicals used in mothballs to kill and repel insects might not be very good for humans, either.

Mothballs are made of white crystals of two **very dangerous chemicals**, para-dichlorobenzene (1,4-dichlorobenzene) and/or naphthalene. Both chemicals are solid at room temperature but produce very strong vapors. Mothballs are sold as flakes or pressed into cakes. Both these chemicals are fumigants and must be present in high concentration to be effective; herein lies the problem. Concentrations high enough to be effective for insect control can be dangerous for anyone exposed to them.

Mothballs are used mainly to ward off insect pests that damage clothes, such as carpet beetles and clothes moths (chapter 5), and as a deterrent to some landscape pests. They are often used in excess, which exposes people to these hazardous compounds. Para-dichlorobenzene may be a carcinogen and may also damage the liver and kidneys at high doses. Naphthalene can damage your liver and cause eye injury.

There are better ways to protect fabrics in storage from insect attack (see chapter 5). *There is no good reason to risk your health by using mothballs now that we know better.*

If mothballs *are* used, however—and no matter what I write here, some people will continue to use them—they should only be used sparingly, and anything stored around mothballs should be thoroughly cleaned before being worn. Dry-clean wool and silk articles, and wash other fabrics, to remove all mothball smell before wearing them.

Internet resources:

www.livingwithbugs.com/mothball.html

Electronic pest-control devices

"Send me $29.95 in the next thirty minutes and I'll send you a device, about the size of a deck of cards, that plugs into any wall outlet and will eliminate all insect pests, and even mice, from your home! Do it today and I'll send you two for the price of one!" If you've read much of this book, you're smart enough to know that this claim is ridiculous—but this is exactly the offer made by some manufacturers of ultrasonic or electronic pest-control devices.

In recent years, a number of devices have come on the market that claim to kill or repel pests by some combination of ultrasonic high-pitched sound and electromagnetic radiation. These devices are usually lumped into the category of electronic pest-control devices. It would be great if one simple device solved all your pest-control needs. But, like the old saying says: *"If it sounds too good to be true, it probably isn't true."*

Electronic pest-control devices come in several types. Some claim to repel pest insects, spiders, and rodents by ultrasonic, or very high-pitched, sound. Others claim to produce an electro-magnetic field that acts as a repellent, while newer devices add ionic air cleaning. Typically the small devices are plugged directly into electric wall outlets or through an adapter cord. The claim is that the devices drive pests out of a room, or structure, by a combination of electromagnetic, sonic and/or ultrasonic energy. The idea is that high energy waves are repellent to the various pests—everything from cockroaches to mice.

Do they work? Probably not. But surprisingly they have not been tested extensively by either the scientific community or the manufacturers themselves. In my experience these two groups have very different reasons for not testing something. Scientists, especially those at universities, have very limited resources with which to do research, and so projects are carefully screened. Projects that are deemed unlikely to produce results don't get much time or money devoted to them. Manufacturers, on the other hand, typically have more resources to devote to research, so a lack of attention to a particular problem must have another explanation. In my experience, the reason manufacturers neglect to test a particular product is because they are afraid it might not perform up to expectations. In short, *if it is never tested, it can never fail*.

The short answer is that none of these devices has been scientifically shown to do what it claims to do. There are a few published scientific studies, but these have generally concentrated on a very specific effect such as the number of eggs produced by insects exposed to ultrasonic sound versus egg production in those which were not exposed. The studies have only very limited usefulness for predicting how effective the devices might be for general pest control.

I believe that if manufacturers had scientific data that demonstrated that their devices work, they would make it easily available. Unfortunately such data is not available. Instead, testimonials are the only evidence of their efficacy that is offered. Testimonial data alone is simply not reliable because it is highly subject to the placebo effect, which, in the simplest terms, means that people see what they want to see. For example, if you have just spent $29.95 on a newfangled pest-control device, you may swear you see an effect, whether or not the effect is real.

Internet resources:

www.livingwithbugs.com/electron.html

Biorational ("eco-friendly") pesticides

I consider this to be one of the most important sections of the book. Sooner or later *almost everyone* will resort to using a pesticide to control some pest around their home. The type of pesticide you choose to use at these times can make a big difference in terms of your impact on the environment and the overall health of your family. It is sort of like the fast food and diet debate: you can choose quick and inexpensive, but not very nutritious; or you can choose to put a little more effort and expense into the selections but end up with a big difference in terms of your health.

Pesticides are chemicals that kill pests or disrupt pest populations. Insecticides are pesticides that target insect pests, herbicides are pesticides that target weeds, and fungicides target disease-causing fungi. Even more specific categories are sometimes used, such as termiticide (termites), acaricide (mites), and so on. A pest is defined as an organism (plant, animal, fungus, or microbe) that causes some type of damage or loss to something we value. Pesticides can be further grouped in a number of different categories such as synthetic pesticides, organic pesticides, inorganic pesticides and biorational pesticides. This can be very confusing and may seem completely irrelevant, except that these groupings can tell you a lot about how a particular pesticide works and also provide some indication about how toxic it may for the user.

Synthetic pesticides have only been around for about sixty years, since the end of World War II. Synthetic pesticides are developed in laboratories and manufactured in chemical plants. Familiar examples of synthetic pesticides are DDT, Roundup™,

Sevin™, Diazinon™, and Dursban™. These pesticides are very effective and inexpensive, and until recently they were widely used in agriculture and around homes. However, "synthetics" have two characteristics that make them less desirable today: they are **not very pest-specific** and they are **very persistent in the environment**. Both characteristics lead to harmful effects on non-target and non-pest species because they kill indiscriminately. In addition, the negative effects last a long time. Manufacturers of pesticides are now emphasizing the development of new classes of compounds that are more pest-specific and less persistent in the environment.

Not all synthetic pesticides are bad. Insect growth regulators (IGRs) are compounds, sometimes natural but sometimes synthetic, that disrupt the development of an insect, usually preventing immature stages from becoming adults. IGRs generally affect only target pests or other closely related insects and are considered both relatively safe and environmentally friendly.

Organic pesticides are compounds made by other plants, animals, or microbes. Often these are compounds that the plant or animal uses to protect itself from the same "pests." One of the best examples of an organic pesticide is nicotine, derived from tobacco leaves. Tobacco leaves make nicotine as a defense against insects that eat tobacco. Since nicotine is so poisonous to most insects and mites, very few are able to exploit tobacco as a food resource. Years ago, farmers and gardeners learned how to extract nicotine from tobacco leaves and use it as a natural, organic pesticide. Even today some gardeners swear by **tobacco tea** as a general purpose organic insecticide (google "tobacco tea" for more information).

Other organic pesticides include **rotenone**, made from the roots of certain tropical plants; **neem oil,** made from the seeds of the tropical neem tree; **rosemary and peppermint oils**, essential oils of those plants; and many others. The key thing to remember about organic pesticides is that *just because they are organic does not mean they are non-toxic or even low-toxicity.* Nicotine and

Biorational insecticides available to homeowners

Insecticidal soap is the biorational pesticide most widely used by gardeners and commercial growers overall. Insecticidal soap is a type of highly refined soap that has insecticidal properties (i.e. kills pests) but at the same time does not harm landscape or crop plants if used correctly. Ordinary household soaps can be used as a crude insecticide, but you run the risk of injuring plants to which they are applied because of impurities in all-purpose soaps. Insecticidal soap is available as a concentrate that should be mixed with water to a 1–2% concentration (approximately 1–2 oz of soap concentrate per gallon of water). Insecticidal soap is very effective against soft-bodied pests like **aphids, spider mites**, and **scale insect crawlers** that feed on plant leaves. Insecticidal soap can be used outdoors in the garden as well as on indoor houseplants. In fact, insecticidal soap is one of the very few insecticides I would ever use indoors.

Unfortunately, some people believe that insecticidal soap burns leaves and won't use it for this reason. If soaps are used correctly, however, they won't harm plants. First, be sure to use **fresh soap concentrate** when mixing solutions. As any liquid soap concentrate ages it oxidizes and turns brown, like an old banana. If you mix old, oxidized concentrate with water it produces a milky precipitate that *can* burn plants. Fresh soap won't become milky and won't harm plants. (See the Internet resources for a simple "freshness" test you can do.) Second, I always suggest that soaps be used as a **leaf wash**. Thoroughly wet the plant with water, apply soap solution to all surfaces, wait 30 minutes, then rinse with water. Do this in the morning so the plant has a chance to dry completely before nightfall.

Neem oil and other botanical insecticides are products of plants. Plants produce these chemicals for their own defense against plant-feeding insects and plant diseases. Neem oil is made by the tropical neem tree. This natural oil has been used for hundreds of years and is very effective for stopping insects from feeding on plants. Like insecticidal soap, neem oil concentrate is mixed with water and applied to garden plants to stop leaf-feeding beetles and similar insect pests. Other plant-based insecticides include essential ➔

➤ oils such as clove oil, geraniol (geranium), and peppermint oil.

Insect growth regulators (IGR) are compounds that interfere with the development, or growth, of insects from the egg stage to the adult insect. An insect growth regulator will usually target a specific stage, such as preventing larvae from developing into adults. Larvae that are exposed to IGRs eventually die. For example, the insect growth regulator **methoprene** prevents larval fleas from completing development to the biting adult stage. IGRs interrupt the normal life cycle of the pest without adversely affecting other organisms. Very effective insecticides containing IGRs are now available for fleas, cockroaches, termites, mosquitoes, and some nuisance ants.

Microbial pesticides are either live insect pathogens (organisms that cause disease) or products of microbes that cause sickness in insects. Microbial pesticides are very specific to insect pests and cause no disease or injury in other organisms, including us. Examples of microbial pesticides are *Bacillus thurengiensis* (various strains) and spinosad, a fermentation product of certain soil microbes.

rotenone, for example, can be highly toxic compounds.

Inorganic pesticides are natural compounds from the earth, not made by a plant, animal, or microbe. Often these compounds are mined or otherwise extracted from minerals. **Boric acid**, or borate, is probably the best example in wide use today. Boric acid is highly toxic to insects but relatively low in toxicity to mammals. It is widely used as a wood preservative against insect and fungal attack as well as in poison baits, in addition to many other industrial applications. Boric acid is mined as a mineral called **borate** (also called borax) made famous by the *Twenty-Mule Team Borax* wagons that hauled borate across the Mojave Desert in the 1880s. Other, far more toxic inorganic pesticides include arsenic, copper, and sulfur.

The term **biorational (or "eco-friendly") pesticide** does not refer to a separate category of pesticides but rather includes those synthetic, organic, or inorganic ones that exhibit both **low mammalian toxicity** and **very low environmental impact**. In other words, they are both relatively safe for the user and do not adversely impact species for which they are not intended. Biorational pesticides include **plant oils, soaps, microbial pesticides** (such as *Bacillus thurengiensis*, spinosad, entomopathogenic nematodes), and **insect growth regulators**. When used correctly, biorational pesticides are just as effective as conventional pesticides and they should always be your first choice.

Internet resources:

www.livingwithbugs.com/organic.html
www.livingwithbugs.com/soap.html (insecticidal soap)
www.livingwithbugs.com/neem.html (neem oil insecticide)
www.livingwithbugs.com/spinosad.html (spinosad insecticide)
www.livingwithbugs.com/botanical_insecticide.html (insecticides made from plants)

Buying pest-control (exterminator) services

Most of the time you don't need professional pest-control services to solve simple pest or nuisance problems around the home. You can skip the periodic maintenance treatments that are often sold at monthly intervals. The pest-control industry does not want to hear that but it is true: if you are willing to spend a little time and sometimes get a little dirty, most people can do their own pest control around the house. The advantages of this do-it-yourself approach are twofold: you'll save money, and you may even be able to accomplish the same level of pest control and protection for your home and family with less harmful impacts on your health and the environment. In a sense that is what this book is about: helping you protect home and health by focusing on what is important and ignoring what may be less important.

Even though you can do most things yourself, however,

occasionally you may need the services of a pest-control company to perform more complex operations or services that involve specialized equipment. Examples of pest-control situations that the average homeowner should not attempt themselves include treatments for **subterranean termites, structure fumigation,** and some treatments for **carpenter ants.** When you do need to hire someone, use the following as your guide:

(1) Select a company based on their reputation, how long they have been in the community, and their willingness to answer your questions. The last point is especially important. They should give you written material that describes the problem they propose to treat and how they propose to treat it, including what chemicals will be used and in what amounts.

(2) Companies differ in the range of pest situations that they routinely handle. This is especially true for less common pests, like bed bugs, or for situations that require specialized equipment, like some termite applications and structure fumigation. Ask if they have experience with the pest-control situation for which you need service.

(3) Do not select a pest-control company based on price alone, an advertisement in the phone book, or the "deal of the week." Be cautious of unsolicited sales pitches and never select a given treatment just because your neighbor's property is being treated or because there is "leftover spray from another job."

(4) Ask for references from previous clients, and check them.

(5) Don't be pressured into an immediate decision. No pest situation requires immediate treatment. In most cases, a delay of a few days or weeks won't make any difference whatsoever. Take time to gather information and make a good decision.

(6) Be cautious of claims of "secret formulations" or negative comments about competitors. Also be cautious of claims of endorsement by local government or university personnel, as these folks are generally not permitted to make recommendations about specific companies or products.

(7) There is no need to treat outdoors for insects during the winter months, since insects are inactive when it is cold. Tropical and semi-tropical climates, including parts of the southeastern US, may be the exception here.

(8) An adult should be at home when pest-control treatments are carried out, to answer questions about the property.

(9) Maintenance treatments, often suggested for intervals of one to three months, are not necessary, although in certain specific cases—such as Formosan termite control in tropical climates, where pest pressure and damage potential are especially high—repeat treatments may be justified.

(10) Tenting and fumigation of residential structures is almost never necessary for pests other than drywood termites. Fumigation is sometimes appropriate for commercial structures like warehouses, however, where access to stored products can be difficult.

Internet resources:

www.livingwithbugs.com/sel_pco.html

Appendix
Identifying an unknown bug

So, some little critter has been bugging you. Now that you've got it firmly in hand, or maybe in a jar, what's next? This book can help you deal with lots of little creepy-crawlers, but what if you have no idea what it is? The following charts, or keys, will help you identify your unknown bug.

All keys for scientific names divide things into groups, which are then divided into further subgroups, logically based on **similar, or shared, characteristics**. The groups are arranged in the order: Kingdom, Phylum, Class, Order, Family, Genus, and Species. Everything covered here is in the Animal Kingdom in the Phylum Arthropoda (see chapter 1). When you see the scientific name of something, whether it be animal or plant, it is the **genus** and **species** that make up the scientific name. The genus name is capitalized, the species name is not, and the whole name is usually italicized or underlined; for example: *Musca domestica,* the house fly.

This key is different. Scientific keys end up counting hairs on legs and that's not a reasonable demand in this situation. Here we list twenty-two common "bugs" found around homes, giving a common name, size, description, where they are commonly found, notes on relevant activities or habits and what time of year they are found, plus a simple drawing of their overall shape. The drawings are simple outlines with distracting details left out. Look for an identifying feature of your specimen in the descriptions and drawings below. If nothing looks familiar, perhaps the critter just hitched a ride into the house and is trying to get back outside with the least amount of trouble. But if you find something that seems to match, go to the relevant chapter to learn more.

Ants (see nuisance ants or carpenter ants)

Bed Bugs
Order: Hemiptera; chapter 1

Size: small, about ¼" long

Description: Bed bugs are flat and wide, roughly the shape of a watermelon seed but smaller; their color is a mahogany brown; they do not have wings.

Where found: Bed bugs' narrow bodies allow them to hide in very tight places, such as cracks, crevices, and under the edges of wallpaper or the edge of a mattress; they hide near where they feed.

Period of Activity: Since they are indoors, they can be active during all seasons of the year.

Notes: A sign of the presence of bed bugs is a sweet odor that permeates a badly infested room; another sign is the dark splatter of feces they leave behind on a mattress; they are nocturnal, feeding/ biting at night while their host is asleep.

Boxelder bugs
Order: Hemiptera; chapter 8

Adult size: Medium, ½–¾" long

Description: Dull black; oval shape with a thin, red "X" across the back; their wings fold down over the back and the red lines are formed by the folded wings.

Where found: Outdoors in the spring and summer in maple and boxelder trees; in the fall and winter they amass on the siding of houses or the bark of large trees in search of an overwintering site, which may be in the attic or living areas of your house.

Period of Activity: Seasonal activities vary; see above.

Notes: Once they have found a spot to overwinter, they just wait for spring before becoming active again.

Carpenter ants
Order: Hymentoptera; chapter 2

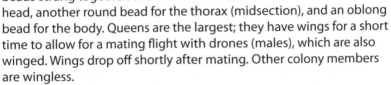

Adult size: Medium to large, ⅜–1" long, depending upon caste status and general health of the colony.

Description: Usually shiny black or a combination of red and black in color, these are the largest ants found in homes in the US. Ants are slender insects, with the look of 3 beads strung together: a round bead for the head, another round bead for the thorax (midsection), and an oblong bead for the body. Queens are the largest; they have wings for a short time to allow for a mating flight with drones (males), which are also winged. Wings drop off shortly after mating. Other colony members are wingless.

Where found: Flying or wandering both indoors and outdoors; colonies hollow out places to live in any material from stumps to the wood in our homes.

Period of Activity: The mating flight takes place in spring, after which queens search for new places to start a colony; spring, summer and fall are active months for feeding and colony growth; they are not active in winter.

Notes: Ants marching back and forth in lines of traffic that look like rush hour are a sure sign of trouble. If they are inside, or marching up the side of a building, this is traffic between a nest and its food source; those living outdoors have no need to come inside to search for food. A few ants found wandering about outdoors are just scouting for food.

Chigger mites
Phylum: Arthropoda, Class: Arachnida, Order: Acari; chapter 6

Size: Tiny mite, about the size of a period at the end of a sentence.

Description: A tiny bright red-orange mite; as a larva, the stage that bites people, it has only six legs, but it develops two more as it becomes an adult, ending up with eight; so small that they are not easily seen.

Where found: Chiggers live outdoors in areas of dense vegetation, such as gardens or brushy or wooded areas.

Period of Activity: Warmer seasons of the year; they are more common in the southern parts of the US.

Notes: The side effect of chiggers is much more noticeable than the mite itself; they leave behind multiple, intensely itchy bites; they tend to bite along areas of constricted clothing like the tops of socks, waistbands, etc.; also known as harvest mites.

Clothes moths
Order: Lepidoptera; chapter 5

Adult size: Small moth, ¼" long.

Description: A plain, straw-colored moth; it has no distinctive color markings, but does have a "feathered" fringe at the bottom of its wings; the larval stage is a cream-colored caterpillar, also small.

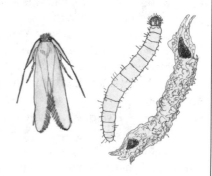

Where found: Adult moths are seldom seen, preferring to stay in the dark (for example, in the back of the closet); larvae will be found wherever they are feeding.

Period of Activity: Any time.

Notes: Larvae feed on anything containing animal hair protein, such as feathers, wool, and fur. Larvae may take on the color of whatever they are infesting. Besides making holes in fabric, some clothes moth larvae make webbing; others weave silken "tubes" which they use for shelter.

Cluster flies
Order: Diptera; chapter 8

Adult size: Medium, ⅜–½" long.

Description: Generally the size and shape of a house fly. Their most distinctive characteristic is the way they die—as they die, they end up lying upside down, spinning around helplessly in circles propelled by their wings; the buzzing sound this makes often gives away the presence of cluster flies in the room.

Where found: Outdoors—or indoors, where cluster flies can be found flitting around the room, bouncing off the windows or buzzing around in circles upside down.

Period of Activity: Mostly in late summer or fall.

Notes: More common where there is an abundance of earthworms.

Cockroaches
Order: Dictyoptera; chapter 4

Adult size: Medium to large (½"–2"), depending on species.

Description: Generally oval shaped, flat bodied, with long legs and long antennae; head is concealed from above as if they are wearing a hood; those that have wings carry them folded down over the body; brown to black in color.

Where found: Indoors, anywhere food is available including crumbs, cooking grease, etc.

Period of Activity: Active indoors all year round.

Notes: Can run very fast.

Drain flies (moth flies)
Order: Diptera; chapter 8

Adult size: Small, ⅛" long

Description: Imagine a tiny gnat wearing a fur coat that covers even their wings—that's a drain fly; when not in flight they carry their wings folded down over their body, roof-like, which makes them look like moths.

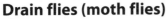

Where found: Indoors in areas where it can be damp, such as near the sink or tub in bathrooms, kitchens, or laundry rooms; damp greenhouses are a favorite spot; outdoors in moist and shady spots like compost bins or bogs; anywhere there is something wet or slimy.

Period of Activity: Outdoors in the warmer seasons; indoors, drain flies can be active all year.

Notes: Drain flies are found in very similar spots to fungus gnats; since they are both very small, the easiest way to tell them apart is that fungus gnats are more delicate, like a mosquito, while drain flies are hairy and look more like tiny moths.

Fleas

Order: Siphonaptera; chapter 1

Adult size: Tiny, about ¹⁄₁₆" long.

Description: Fleas have no wings; they have long legs, for jumping; their body is very flat side to side, enabling them to weave their way quickly through dense fur, it also makes them very difficult to catch; adult fleas are dark in color; flea larvae are small, cream-colored and worm-like in appearance.

Where found: Fleas are ectoparasites of dogs, cats, and their human associates; there are many species of fleas but most are limited to very specific hosts. Adult cat fleas will be found on cats or dogs and the bed of the infested animal; they could also be found on a person in a badly infested home; the larval stage will be found only in the bedding of the pet, but their small size makes them difficult to spot.

Period of Activity: Fleas are more active in the warm months of the year.

Notes: An indication of an infestation is flea dirt, little dark flecks of dried blood that fleas excrete; flea dirt can be found by combing through an infested pet's fur.

Flour and dermestid beetles

Order: Coleoptera; chapter 4

Adult size: Small, about ¹⁄₈" long

Description: Tiny beetles with hardened wing coverings; flour beetles are reddish brown, slender and flat; dermestids are wider and more oval shaped, with colors ranging from gray to black and variations in between, including some with black-and-white markings; as with all beetles, the larvae are soft-bodied grubs; flour beetle larvae are cream-colored; dermestid larvae are about the size and shape of a grain of rice but are covered with bristly hair; some species are "hairier" than others.

Where found: Larvae infest food such as flour, cereal, dry pet food, birdseed, spices, etc.

Period of Activity: Any time of the year

Notes: The presence of flour beetles in flour can cause it to turn a dirty gray color; carpet beetles infest wool carpets—the usual sign is the carpet becoming threadbare, especially in darkened corners or where draperies hang low above the carpet; dermestid beetles shed their larval skins and the "cast" skins can be found lying in the vicinity of the infestation.

Fruit flies (see vinegar flies)

Fungus gnats

Order: Diptera; chapter 8

Size: Tiny, about 1/16".

Description: Very delicate flies with small bodies, long legs, and transparent wings; they look a little bit like tiny mosquitoes—without the annoying whine.

Where found: Flying around or sitting on/near damp areas with lots of decaying organic matter, such as compost bins or over-watered houseplants; the larval stage—tiny, white maggots—can be found in the compost or in the soil of houseplants.

Period of Activity: Usually in the warmer seasons, unless in a controlled environment like a greenhouse or indoors around houseplants, where they may be active all year.

Notes: They are so small that a few individuals would not get much notice, but when the populations build, a person working around houseplants, for example, could raise a "cloud" of these gnats.

Hard ticks

Phylum: Arthropoda, Class: Arachnida, Order: Acari; chapter 1

Adult size: Small to medium, up to about 1/4" long when fully fed (engorged).

Description: Not an insect, a tick has eight legs, like a spider; a fully fed tick looks much different than one that hasn't fed; before feeding, a tick has an oval, flat body and its legs sit out to the side of its body, almost like a crab's; after feeding, a tick's body swells to a soft, ballooned version of the unfed tick's, and its head and legs are barely visible compared to the rest of its body; color is tan/brown to black.

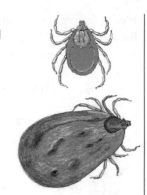

Where found: In tall grass, brush, rodent dens; moving around on or attached to dogs, cats, or people.

Period of Activity: Any time it is not too cold—basically any time it is above freezing.

Notes: A swollen tick attached to a pet can easily be mistaken for a wart protruding through the fur; close examination reveals legs sticking out from under the swollen body.

Head lice

Order: Anoplura; chapter 1

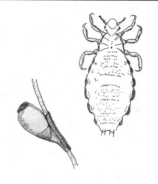

Adult size: Small, about ⅛" long.

Description: Light or dark depending on whether they have recently fed, head lice are narrow-bodied insects with a head that is narrower than their thorax (mid-section); their legs are built for grabbing onto hair shafts; eggs (nits) are longer than they are wide, with a translucent appearance; eggs are glued onto hair shafts close to the scalp.

Where found: Head lice are found normally on heads, as you would expect, moving between the scalp where they feed and the hair where they lay their eggs and cement them to the shafts; occasionally they can be found on combs or hair brushes, and on hats or other apparel worn on the head.

Period of Activity: Active in all seasons.

Notes: One of the first signs of head-lice infestation is a lot of head-scratching, as their bite produces an itchy wound; empty nit cases "move" down the hair away from the scalp as the hair grows; the white color of the empty nit case is more easily seen in the hair than the darker, nit-occupied case while it is still close to the scalp.

Hornets (see social wasps)

House flies

Order: Diptera; chapter 8

Adult size: Small, about ¼" long.

Description: Grayish-colored flies with stripes behind the head; often associated with decaying animal or vegetable matter (garbage, manure, or compost); large numbers of house flies often indicate a problem with waste disposal of one kind or another.

Where found: Outdoors, around waste disposal sites.

Period of Activity: Activity peaks during warm months.

Notes: There are a number of flies that look similar—house flies, face flies, cluster flies, stable flies, and others; the best way to tell them apart is by their behavior rather than size or coloration.

Ladybird beetles (ladybugs)

Order: Coleoptera; chapter 8

Adult size: Small, ⅛–¼" long.

Description: Rounded bodies with hardened shells over their wings; many color combinations from various shades of red, to orange with black dots, to black with red dots; the larval stage looks nothing like the adult—larvae are orange to reddish and black with a "corrugated" soft body resembling a tiny alligator; the adults look like tiny Volkswagen Beetle™ autos.

Where found: Outdoors in the garden, feasting on small insects—usually where there are high populations of pests that they use for food, such as aphids; some species look for overwintering sites in houses, so they gather on exterior walls looking for a way inside; in spring they may gather inside, at the windows, looking for a way out.

Period of Activity: Warm seasons.

Notes: Their tiny eggs are light yellow, football-shaped, and set together on end like bowling pins; they can be found on leaf surfaces wherever adults are found.

Meal moths

Order: Lepidoptera; chapter 4

Adult size: Small, about ⅜" long.

Description: When at rest their wings are folded down over their body, making them look long and thin; in this position they have a distinct broad band of dark brown across their wings, the rest being gray; larvae are small cream-colored caterpillars with a dark head capsule; larvae leave fine webbing behind in the material that they infest.

Where found: Larvae infest foods, most commonly cereals, nuts, grains, dried fruit, bird seed, etc.; adults can be found flitting around the house, perhaps close to the infested area.

Period of Activity: Any time of the year

Notes: The webbing left by the caterpillars often collects and holds the infested food together, leaving clumps clinging to the edge of a box or bag.

Mosquitoes

Order: Diptera; chapter 1

Adult size: Small, delicate flies about ¼" long.

Description: Mosquitoes make a distinctive whining sound, produced by their wings; these blood-feeders are persistent biters that often occur in the evening, before sunset.

Where found: Outdoors; more common around bodies of still water like lakes and ponds.

Period of Activity: Warm months, but some species are active at cool temperatures at higher elevations.

Notes: Mosquitoes transmit a variety of important diseases; insect repellents provide effective protection against mosquito bites.

Nuisance ants

Order: Hymenoptera; chapter 4

Adult size: Small, ⅛–¼" long.

Description: Small, dark-brown to amber, or even yellow-colored ants; they make colonies in homes or in soil surrounding homes, enter homes in search of food and water, and become a nuisance.

Where found: Indoors where food and water are available.

Period of Activity: Indoor activity peaks in spring and summer.

Notes: Large colonies containing thousands of worker ants in walls and ceilings can be difficult to control.

Paper wasps (see social wasps)

Silverfish and firebrats

Order: Thysanura; chapter 8

Adult size: Medium, ½–¾" long.

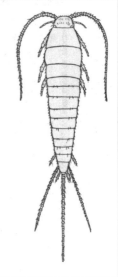

Description: Slender body, tapering toward the ends, with two long antennae on the front and three long "tails" on the rear; silvery gray to brown in color; no wings.

Where found: Silverfish are usually found in damp places, whereas firebrats favor drier habitats; they can be on walls or ceilings; they like to infest paper or books in storage.

Period of Activity: Can be found indoors at any time of year.

Notes: Can move very quickly and jump by flipping themselves up into the air.

Social wasps

Order: Hymenoptera; chapter 3

Adult size: Medium, ½–¾" long.

Description: Medium-sized wasps, often with yellow and black coloration; they create large, papery nests suspended above ground or buried in a cavity below ground; sometimes aggressive in defense of the nest; may swarm and sting multiple times; some species are pests at outdoor events that include exposed food.

Where found: Outdoors.

Period of Activity: Nest construction begins in the spring and continues throughout summer; nests are abandoned in early winter; maximum activity is usually at the end of summer.

Notes: In the US, social wasps are called yellowjackets, paper wasps, and hornets.

Termites

Order: Isoptera; chapter 2

Size: Small to medium-sized, about ¼–½" long, except for the queens, which can be larger.

Description: Worker termites are cream-colored; they are often described as "white ants," though they are not related to ants and their body shape is more stout, lacking the thin waist of an ant. Queens have large, smoky-gray transparent wings that are used in the mating flight; the wings drop off shortly afterwards, and from then on queens are wingless.

Where found: In flight (for the mating flight only) out-doors or indoors, wandering indoors or outdoors (after the mating flight, in search of a new colony), or inside their colony (termites eat wood, so they don't ever have to leave the colony except to expand it or start a new one); colonies can be inside of any piece of wood, for certain species especially if it is in contact with moisture.

Period of Activity: Since they are insulated inside of wood, they can be active most of the year, unless it gets very cold.

Notes: Some termites can expand their territory by building "mud shelter tubes" up from the soil and across barriers to dry timbers; inspecting for these mud tubes is therefore important in detecting the presence of certain termites.

Ticks (see hard ticks)

Vinegar flies/small "fruit flies"/pomace flies
Order: Diptera; chapter 8

Adult size: Small, ⅛" long.

Description: Amber flies, often with prominent red eyes.

Where found: Often seen hovering around ripening fruit on kitchen counters; anywhere fresh fruit is kept, or near compost bins; they can also be a nuisance around home pickling.

Period of Activity: Most common in late summer and fall, when lots of fresh fruit is around.

Notes: These are the flies many people are familiar with from "fruit fly" genetics studies in biology class.

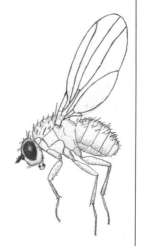

Yellowjacket wasps (see social wasps)

Identifying insect damage

At times you may not recognize an insect, or its damage, but you know something is wrong. The following is a list of scenarios describing common insect activities or damage symptoms, and signs of their presence. The insect or insects that could be the cause are then identified, and directions given to where more information may be found. These examples are drawn from my experience answering questions from homeowners over the last twenty years.

In food or areas where food is stored or prepared

There are fine webs with bits of cereal/crumbs, etc. dangling along the edges of my cereal box/liner of my cake mix box/inside the dog-food bag, etc. ➤ MEAL MOTHS (chapter 4)

There are things like bristly grains of rice inside my kitchen cupboards/in the dog-food bag/in my packaged foods, etc. Some of them look like empty shells; others are moving. ➤ **DERMESTID BEETLES** (chapter 4)

I don't use my flour very often, and when I looked in the bag the flour was gray instead of white. ➤ **FLOUR BEETLES** (chapter 4)

My flour has small, reddish-brown things in it that look like they might be moving. ➤ **FLOUR BEETLES** (chapter 4)

There are moths flitting about my kitchen/pantry/the closet where the bird feed is stored; they are small, tan moths with a dark-brown band across their wings. ➤ **MEAL MOTHS** (chapter 4)

I opened the pantry door last night and these medium-sized bugs with long antennae went scuttling back into the shadows. ➤ **COCKROACHES** (chapter 4)

My flour has tiny, white, worm-like things in it. ➤ **FLOUR BEETLES** (chapter 4), or **DERMESTID BEETLES** (chapter 4), or **MEAL MOTHS** (chapter 4)

There are very tiny flies hovering around my kitchen near the bananas/apples/fruit, which are getting over-ripe. ➤ **VINEGAR FLIES** (chapter 8)

I'm making pickles in my kitchen and the pickles need to sit out to cure in their brine. Tiny flies always seem to be in the vicinity. ➤ **VINEGAR FLIES** (chapter 8)

There are lines of small ants parading in and out of my kitchen/bedrooms/storage pantry. ➤ **NUISANCE ANTS** (chapter 4); If the ants are larger (¼" or more) ➤ **CARPENTER ANTS** (chapter 2)

Indoors or outdoors near potting soil or compost

My houseplants are under grow-lights for the winter, so I like to keep them watered. When I water them, a cloud of gnat-like insects rises up and gets in my face. ➤ **FUNGUS GNATS** or **DRAIN/MOTH FLIES** (chapter 8)

Tiny, fuzzy-looking flying insects always seem to be present around my sink in the kitchen/bathroom/laundry room. ➤ **DRAIN/MOTH FLIES** (chapter 8)

When I open the compost bin, I raise a cloud of tiny little flying insects. ✦ **FUNGUS GNATS** or **DRAIN/MOTH FLIES** (chapter 8)

When cleaning the gutters on the house, I see lots of little insects flying around. ✦ **FUNGUS GNATS** or **DRAIN/MOTH FLIES** (chapter 8)

I find long, many-legged creatures curled up in the top of my house-plant flower pots, or sometimes down inside the pots. ✦ **MILLIPEDES** (try googling millipedes)

Sometimes when I stir the compost, these long, red creatures with many, long legs race around the compost. They're kind of scary looking. ✦ **CENTIPEDES** (try googling centipedes)

Indoors on fabrics, hides, and other non-food items

My grandmother's favorite feathered hat has been stored in the attic. When we took it out to look at it, the feathers have been destroyed. ✦ **DERMESTID BEETLES** or **CLOTHES MOTHS** (chapter 5)

Dad's pride and joy, his six-point trophy mounted elk head hanging in the parlor, has started losing its hair in small spots. ✦ **DERMESTID BEETLES** or **CLOTHES MOTHS** (chapter 5)

Holes have been forming in our wool carpet/rug, especially where it is hidden under the furniture or beneath the drapes. ✦ **CLOTHES MOTHS** or **DERMESTID BEETLES** (chapter 5)

Our wool shirts/sweaters/blankets had small holes in the fabric when we got them out of storage. ✦ **CLOTHES MOTHS** or **DERMESTID BEETLES** (chapter 5)

When I took my children's high-school insect collections out to show them to our grandchildren, the insects were all falling apart. ✦ **DERMESTID BEETLES** (chapter 5)

We saved a lot of seed from our garden the last few years. Now there are fine webs inside the packages with seeds hanging from them. ✦ **MEAL MOTHS** (chapter 4)

We stored some old books and magazines out in the garage. When we opened them recently there were holes tunneled through the pages. ✦ **SILVERFISH** or **TERMITES** (chapter 4)

I had a poster hanging on the inside of my apartment door. I noticed creepy-looking bugs running to hide behind the poster. When I took it down, there were more bugs on the back of the poster and the paper looked like it was being scraped off the poster. ➤ **SILVERFISH** (chapter 4)

Going through old books and papers, I found all the book bindings were tattered and chewed. ➤ **COCKROACHES** or **SILVERFISH** (chapter 4)

Indoors—general

It's autumn and there are lots of flies bouncing around the windows. Some of them end up lying upside down, spinning around, buzzing their wings against the floor. ➤ **CLUSTER FLIES** (chapter 8)

There are long, thin, cylindrical things with oodles of legs lying curled up on the top of the soil in my flowerpots. ➤ **MILLIPEDES** (try googling millipedes)

In the spring, there are hundreds or thousands of little, round, red bugs with black spots flying around the windows of the house/garage. They started arriving in the fall, and we found them everywhere, crawling around, falling off the ceiling, getting into everything. ➤ **LADYBUGS/ LADYBIRD BEETLES** (chapter 8)

In the spring, there are hundreds or thousands of medium-sized gray bugs with red X's across their backs flying around the windows of the house/garage. In the fall they had first congregated on the exterior walls, then managed to get inside and we found them everywhere, crawling around, falling off the ceiling, getting into everything. ➤ **BOXELDER BUGS** (chapter 8)

There are rows of ants busily marching along the windowsills, up and down the walls, and across the floor. It looks like a highway for ant traffic. ➤ Small ants: **NUISANCE ANTS** (chapter 4) or larger ants: **CARPENTER ANTS** (chapter 2)

We just checked into a hotel. There is a very odd, sweet smell in the room. When we pulled the sheets off the mattress, there were small, dark, greasy spots on the mattress. ➤ **BED BUGS** (chapter 1)

Living in and/or damaging wood or other building material

I noticed small holes, from pinhole-sized to about the diameter of a pencil lead, appearing in: [pick one] the wood siding on my house, the wood paneling in the den, the oak floor in the living room, wooden kitchen-cabinet doors, my antique kitchen table, my imported wooden jewelry box, etc. Near these holes is a tiny pile of fine sawdust. ➤ **POWDERPOST BEETLES** (chapter 2)

Walking through one of the rooms of my house, I noticed that the floor seems springy under my feet where before it had been quite solid. ➤ **CARPENTER ANTS or TERMITES** (chapter 2)

Outside in the yard I noticed a stream of ants traveling up and down the trunk of a large tree that overhangs the roof. In fact, some of the branches are touching the roof. ➤ **CARPENTER ANTS** (chapter 2)

There are some fair-sized ants in a steady parade marching up and down the corner posts/foundation wall/siding of my house. ➤ **CARPENTER ANTS** (chapter 2)

Repairing some rotted wood around a leaky tub, I broke into a board and it was filled with small bugs. They look like ants, but they seem kind of soft and are a creamy-white color. ➤ **TERMITES** (chapter 2)

Doing an inspection under my house, I saw something that looked almost like roots made of mud growing up over the foundation walls to the sub-floor. When I knocked them off, I discovered these "roots" were hollow. ➤ **TERMITES** (chapter 2)

In the late summer or early fall, swarms of amber-colored insects with long, translucent wings flutter around in the sky. I also find them inside the house, flying around the windows or scurrying around on the floor, especially if their wings have fallen off. ➤ **TERMITES** (chapter 2)

Biting people or pets

My cat/dog is scratching constantly and biting at her skin. When I comb her, the comb picks up a lot of crumbly, dark "dirt." If I drop the "dirt" into water, it dissolves and turns red. ➤ **FLEAS** (chapter 1)

My dog/cat has been doing some scratching. When he lies upside down for a tummy rub, tiny, dark insects can be seen running along the skin underneath the hair. ➤ **FLEAS** (chapter 1)

We just got back from the local park, having at one point walked through some tall grass where there are rodents. I noticed a tiny, dark, almost crab-like bug crawling on my leg. ➤ **TICKS** (chapter 1)

When combing the dog, I noticed a lump, sort of like a big wart, sticking out of her fur where I didn't remember ever seeing one before. ➤ **TICKS** (chapter 1)

I woke up with itchy red bites all over my arms and back. We had not noticed any bugs in our hotel room, but it did have a funny, sweet smell. ➤ **BED BUGS** (chapter 1)

One of our children has been scratching his head a lot. When we examined his head, we found little bumps glued to the side of the hair shafts. ➤ **HEAD LICE** (chapter 1)

Something was tickling my scalp. When I looked in the mirror, I saw something running quickly through my hair. We do have cats and dogs in the house. ➤ **FLEAS** (chapter 1)

I was working in the garden all morning. Now I have some extremely itchy bites in clusters around my legs, where the top of my socks were. ➤ **CHIGGERS** (chapter 6)

Using the Internet

The Internet literally interconnects information from around the world and makes this information available to anyone with a computer. There are good and bad aspects to this. The good news is you now have almost instant access to an immense pool of information. The bad news is you can quickly access an immense pool of unfiltered information—some of this information is good, but some is not so good, and some is even dangerous. The trick is to know how to find what you are looking for, and how to sort the good and useful information from all the rest.

For example, you should be wary of sites that hide or entirely omit the credentials of the author. You should always be able to easily find the author's name and qualifications, usually through an About link, or something similar. If a site publishes articles, or pages, from a variety of sources, each article should include a statement about the author. Also, be wary of sites that display excessive advertising. A good balance might be something like 75% useful content and 25% advertising (though only advertising that is somehow related to the page content).

Another good practice is to check more than one site, especially if the information you seek is important to you. So, if you are wondering when to spray your apple trees for codling moth, for example, you should type the search phase "codling moth + [your state name]" into Google's search engine (www.google.com). If you are lucky, someone will have published a spray calendar that relates to your state, that will tell you exactly when to spray your trees to get the best control. In this case, a university-run site may be better than a commercial site, though this is not always true. Commercial sites are usually updated more often than university sites and tend to have fresher, more current information. Check more than one site, and if the information roughly agrees (say, to within a few days, in the case of codling moth spraying) you can be reasonably confident that the information is accurate. Only rely on a single source if you have a high level of confidence in the reliability of the site and the author.

There are a number of very good online pest and damage image databases. An image database is an organized collection of pictures. In this case, the pictures are of pests and the damage they cause. These databases are best used when you have an idea of what you are looking for and just want to confirm your idea with a picture. The two image databases I turn to most often are BugGuide.net (www.bugguide.net) and Forestry Images (www.forestryimages.org). The BugGuide.net database is a good place to find a picture of a specimen you are trying to identify.

For example, after working through "Identifying an unknown specimen" above, you can log into the BugGuide.net database and often find a picture to compare with your specimen. The Forestry Images database is a joint effort between the University of Georgia and the USDA. I use it most often to find images of wood-boring insects or occasionally pests of landscape plants.

Other sites I use on a more or less regular basis are the Iowa State Entomology Index of Internet Resources (www.ent.iastate.edu/list/), the Bio-Integral Resource Center (www.birc.org), and the University of California IPM Online (www.ipm.ucdavis.edu). The first is a site maintained at Iowa State University and is in some ways the mother of all entomology sites. It is itself an organized collection of links to other sites related to entomology. It is a huge list and many of the entries link to highly specialized sites aimed mainly at professional entomologists. The second is the well known Bio-Integral Resource Center, a non-profit organization that promotes the development of integrated pest management practices. Finally, the University of California State-Wide Integrated Pest Management Program is not just for residents of California. The site delivers a wealth of online, printed, and CD-ROM-based information, as well as images of pests and diseases.

Cooperative Extension and Master Gardeners

Cooperative Extension is an organizational agreement between US states and the federal government to provide research-based information to the general public. The basic idea is to "extend" the knowledge of the university to citizens. Nowadays Extension is organized around offices located in most US counties (county Extension offices) and resources located at land-grant or state universities. Typically, the county tax base maintains the local office and support staff, while federal grants pay for professional staff and research projects.

It is truly unfortunate that more urban homeowners don't know about and use their local county Cooperative Extension personnel. After all, it is their tax dollars that support these offices. Farmers know about Extension because they regularly rely on Extension agents for information about pests, the latest production practices, markets, etc. Most urban dwellers don't know, however, that Extension also has programs for homeowners. Everything from canning and composting to, of course, dealing with insect pests around the home. Many Extension offices use groups of trained volunteers called Master Gardeners to interface with their non-agricultural clients. Master Gardeners are volunteers from the community who agree to serve as Extension's outreach to homeowners (as opposed to the farmers who are Extension's traditional clients), in exchange for a short series of training workshops to get ready to help with a variety of questions. Master Gardeners are trained to refer more technical questions, especially anything involving pesticides, to regular Extension staff.

I urge you to get acquainted with the folks at your local county Extension office and call or visit them to see what they offer. Many Master Gardener programs maintain a clinic, to which unknown pests and diseases can be brought for identification. Most services are free of charge, but check with your local office. You may even decide to get involved with the Master Gardener program for your county and share your own expertise. You can look up the address of your local county Extension office either online (www.extension.org/) or in the phone book under county offices.

Index